Scrapbooks and Broken Strings

Jude Murphy

Scrapbooks and Broken Strings

For Sienna
Because it's all been for Sienna
Always

Scrapbooks and Broken Strings
ISBN 978 1 76109 211 4
Copyright © Jude Murphy 2021
Cover image: Sarah Curry

First published 2021 by
GINNINDERRA PRESS
PO Box 3461 Port Adelaide 5015
www.ginninderrapress.com.au

God be with the mother. As she carried her child may she carry her soul. As her child was born, may she give birth and life and form to her own, higher truth. As she nourished and protected her child, may she nourish and protect her inner life and her independence. For her soul shall be her most painful birth, her most difficult child and the dearest sister to her other children.
Amen.
— Michael Leunig, *Common Prayer Collection*

1

The first thing I need to tell you is that this story doesn't have a 'happy' ending. (Although it's not a tragic one, either.) It doesn't resolve, or tie up nice and neatly, leaving you with the satisfied feeling you might get from, say, the final scene of an Agatha Christie movie. If you don't believe me, feel free to turn to the last chapter, right now, and read it. You'll find it just...pauses. And stops. Because life isn't like that. People's stories don't just end. Well, if people are still alive enough to be writing their stories, then they don't just end. They plod along, generally trying to make sense of all the plodding along that has gone before.

I've read stories by people who can remember their birth. I remember reading one story where a woman claimed to remember her life in utero. To be honest, I'm always pretty sceptical of those claims. I can't remember my birth. And having given birth myself, I believe we're not supposed to remember being born, that we are protected from the memory of such a traumatic event. Even my very early memories are so sketchy I often wonder if I'm making them up, filling in the blanks with my imagination. If I wasn't the spitting image of my mother, I could be forgiven for suspecting I was born into a completely different family. But I do look like my mother. And my father. And my brother. I don't look anything like my sister did, but more of that later.

I know that I was born in 1973 in Nepean Hospital and my parents, Tina and Brendan, brought me home to our house in Werrington, NSW. My brother, Anthony, was four years old. I know that as a kid he had bad bronchitis. I know that we had a dog, a cocker spaniel named Bonnie. There is a photo of Bonnie having a bath in a blue bucket. I know that my mum adored Bonnie, but my dad took her to work one day and someone at the truck yard stole her. I know that my mum was a secretary who always worked, even when we were very little, and my brother and I were looked after by mum's mum, our Mamaļ, the Latvian name for grandmother. I know that my dad was a truck driver with his own company. I know that he was a handsome man who always had a cigarette in his mouth and drank KB beer from a gold-coloured can. I know that he would often disappear for days, even weeks at a time, and that even before my baby sister was born my parents' marriage was on the rocks. But I don't actually remember anything about living in this house in Werrington.

If I had to settle on an earliest memory, it would be in church. I see the scene from the pews upstairs, looking down on the crowd below, and the elevated altar up front. These are the images that flooded my senses every Sunday until my late teenage years, and some weekdays too, when I visited the church with my class, led by the Catholic nuns who taught me through primary school.

So there, taking centre stage, is Christ on the crucifix, looking pretty darn bummed out, his arms spreadeagled, wearing a ragged loincloth with a crown of thorns atop his blood-soaked head. His eyes gaze heavenwards, imploring, I imagine, his maker to explain the purpose of his agony. (I've worn the same expression and begged the same question of my creator many a time. I'm nothing if not melodramatic.)

The church is flooded with rainbow light from the tall, leadlight windows that frame the church's perimeter. More images of Christ dragging a heavy crucifix over his shoulder while helpless women look on, their faces etched with anguish. I will learn soon, from my mother and the nuns, that I am responsible for all this suffering. Apparently, Christ died so that I might live. Apparently, I'm fortunate enough to have been born a Catholic, because although I was born in original sin, I've been baptised, cleansing me of this original sin. Of course, by the time I'm eight years old I will need to sit in a small box with a priest and confess my sins weekly (mortifying crimes such as coveting my sister's doll or allowing my mind to wander during prayer) and as long as I admit my sins and seek forgiveness, I will be absolved. I just need to be careful not to get hit by a bus midweek before I've had a chance to attend confession. In this event, I may be sent straight to the burning fires of hell.

But I digress. Back to the reason we are in church on this particular day. It is my sister's christening, which makes me almost three. I don't remember too much about the ceremony, I've probably filled it in with all my subsequent experience with sacramental ceremonies, but I do remember my mum and dad standing on the altar next to the baptismal bath, an enormous concrete tub full of what I suppose is freezing water, or perhaps acid, given the way babies scream when the priest pours the liquid on their heads.

I'm not supposed to be here. The priest has asked my mum and dad to bring my baby sister up to the altar so that he may chant the sacred incantations and light the sacred candles and christen my sister's head, cleansing her of all the original sin she's been born into. I suspect I've been told, in no uncertain terms, to stay seated in the pew, probably with my older cousins and definitely with my brother, but I've refused. I've followed them up to the altar and I'm standing next to them as they're crowded around the immersing bath. I distinctly remember this part, watching the priest reciting strange riddles and tipping water over my baby sister's head and announcing to the crowd that she was christened that beautiful name to match the beautiful baby girl that she was; Ashlie Jane. I remember the sound of the water washing over her head and splashing in the bath. I remember the flickering flames of the candles and I remember the folds of her pure white christening gown flowing gracefully over my mother's cradling arms. But most of all, I remember feeling jealous of all the attention being paid to my sister. I remember feeling resentful that this day was clearly about her and I was expected to take a back seat. And I remember my mum being angry with me for disobeying her instructions to stay seated and even though the rest of the congregation and the priest and most likely even my dad thought it quite cute that I accompanied everyone up to the altar to be part of my sister's first Catholic sacrament, my mum was livid. I had angered her and disappointed her and had behaved like the huge pain in the arse that I was.

If you're sensing more than a touch of sibling rivalry, you'd be right. I was insanely jealous of my sister from as far back as I can remember. Ashlie the baby. Ashlie the pretty one with her dead-straight, jet-black hair, her wide blue eyes, her cute, upturned nose. Ashlie with the gorgeous name, a name that sounded like the ocean; *Ashlie Jane*. Complete strangers on the street would comment on Ashlie's beauty and completely ignore me, standing right next to her. 'What's your name?' they always asked, sighing and tilting their head in admiration when she told them, always proudly, 'Ashlie Jane,' nodding as if agreeing that her face indeed matched such a pretty name.

I remember one morning Ashlie and I were in bed with Mum. I was lying beside Mum, who held Ashlie in her arms on top of her. Lifting her face and gazing whimsically into her eyes, my mother said, 'Oh Ashlie, you're going to break some hearts someday.'

Innocently I asked my mother, 'Mummy, what about me? Will I break some hearts one day too?'

My mother looked at me, amused. 'Jude,' she laughed. 'I'm sorry, but you can't have beauty and brains.'

Despite this certain knowledge that it sucked to be me, particularly in the face of having a widely adored younger sister, Ashlie and I were inseparable. I don't remember playing with my brother at all, but Ashlie and I spent every minute together. We shared a room. We wore similar clothes. We played with the same toys. Mum cut both our hair boy-short because it was 'more manageable'. (Of course, Ashlie's gorgeous face rocked even the most masculine hairstyle. I, on the other hand, with my tearaway curls and freckled wide nose, was forever being mistaken for a boy.) I know that I would speak for Ashlie because I can remember the teachers and nuns at our primary school always telling me not to. When I remember family holidays, it's always with Ashlie. When I remember walking to and from school, when I remember opening presents on Christmas morning, when I remember Easter egg hunts and trips into my mother's work and visits to our Aunty Vera's house and games of hide-and-seek and swimming in the pool and helping Mum bake chocolate slice and riding in the back seat of Mum's orange Datsun 120Y and going to the St Mary's Band Club to watch a matinee performance of *The Wombles*, it was always with Ashlie. I was forever bossing her around, dressing her up, making her take on the various roles I concocted for her in my games of make-believe; me a teacher, her the student, me the director with the starring role, her the lesser bit part. From the time she was born until I was ten years old, it was always with Ashlie.

And then came 1984.

The tenth of May to be precise.

We were at a paddock that belonged to a man called Charlie, a mate of Dad's. Dad took us there often, and left us there often, where we would run amok in the stables and visit the pig pen and climb trees and, if we were lucky, ride horses. Lord knows what Dad did. It was definitely something to do with making money and almost certainly dodgy, but we didn't care. Strange people came and went, visiting horses that were there on agistment or visiting the family that lived in the house there and I can only imagine how annoying it must have been for them to have a couple of dirt-bruised urchins hanging around, asking a million questions and begging for a ride.

My brother, Anthony, was there sometimes too. But he was a teenager by now, with his own friends getting up to their own no-good. Anthony had a couple of paddock-bashers, old cars and old trail-bikes and he and his mates would drive them around the dirt track at the back of the pig pens, doing burnouts and generally driving recklessly. He had a gun too. A rifle that shot real slugs. I know what the slugs looked like because the day before the day I'm about to tell you about, I saw one lodged in Anthony's hand.

I was in the house, watching Carol (the lady who lived there, the wife of Charlie), straining milk through a nylon stocking. Suddenly a girl named Donna burst through the door. Donna was a little older than me, closer to Anthony's age, and she often hung out with the boys, driving cars and shooting targets. She was actually our neighbour and was also a relative of the family who lived on the property.

'Anthony's been shot!' she announced.

My heart jumped into my throat. I instantly thought she meant he was dead, but a few moments later, Anthony walked through the back door, blood dripping from his hand, a metallic lump sitting beneath the skin. The bullet had entered the skin and travelled a couple of centimetres, now sitting on the back of his hand, just up from his thumb. The relief to see he was still standing turned my legs to jelly.

Carol remained calm, telling him he would need a trip to the hospital. I don't know who took him. Mum would definitely have been at work and Dad wasn't around, but somehow Anthony ended up at the hospital and required surgery the following day.

No one but Anthony and his friend, Paul, really know what happened that day. The initial story was that Paul had fired the gun inside the car and the slug had ricocheted off a surface and into his hand. Later, the story morphed. Apparently, the paddock-basher had run out of fuel and, in frustration, Paul had pointed the rifle at the fuel gauge. Anthony had placed his hand over the gauge, not thinking that Paul would actually pull the trigger. Maybe neither of these stories are anything close to the truth, but it seems the moral of the story is, don't leave teenage boys alone to drive around in cars with guns. I do know Mum and Dad agreed that it would be a good idea to get rid of the gun, and I am certain Mum actually meant it. But I saw that gun, months later, in the boot of Dad's car.

So, the next day, Anthony was in hospital having surgery, the significance of his 'shooting' about to pale in comparison to the following events. Ashlie and I were with Dad, back at the paddock. Mum was at work. This isn't to say that neither of my parents cared whether my brother was in hospital or not. I think that Mum went to work because she couldn't be with my brother anyway, seeing as how he was having surgery. I've also been told that Mum didn't even know we were with Dad. She went off to work thinking that Dad had taken us to a sitter, a woman named Karen who often looked after us after school or in the holidays. But Dad had decided we could come with him and, knowing me, I would have nagged him to let us tag along to the paddock. Dad even picked up a cousin of ours, Kevin, Dad's sister's son, who was the same age as me. And Dad did look after us, in his own way, which meant getting on the grog with his mate and letting the three of us run feral.

I remember a lot about that day. Lots of little details. I remember the blue of Dad's singlet. I remember that Ashlie and I rode a pinto horse named Patches and that Ashlie cantered on him for the first time ever, Patches' hooves clippety-clopping on the dirt driveway. I can smell the mix of saddle leather and horse sweat on my clothes. I remember the feel of the air, autumn cool, and I remember how the sun sat low in the sky as dusk approached, and then, the following details are burned on my brain. It could have happened yesterday. Often it feels like it just happened yesterday.

Dad was drunk. He was sitting with his mate, Charlie, drinking Fosters beer from a blue can. We knew when Dad was full like this, we could ask him for things. We knew we had a better chance of getting what we wanted. And that afternoon, we wanted ice cream.

I need to stop for a moment and explain something here. So up the road from Charlie's paddock was a fruit market, one of those big barns on the side of the highway with wide aisles full of fruit and vegetables, bread and nuts, a fridge full of drinks. Often when we asked Dad for money to buy a drink or a treat, we went to the fruit market. We kids only had to exit the driveway, walk about a hundred metres up a quiet dirt road and we were there. There was rarely any traffic. Across the highway, however, was a petrol station that sold chocolate bars, packets of chips and ice cream. To get there, we had to exit the driveway, but instead of turning left down the quiet, dirt road, we walked straight ahead about a hundred metres up a different dirt road that took us to the highway. And the petrol station, the one with the chocolates and chips and ice cream, was on the other side of that busy highway.

So it was just after five, the sun low in the autumn sky and the air cool on our bare skin. We all wore blue jeans and grubby shirts, dusty sneakers and grimy faces. We all had dirt and horse sweat beneath our fingernails. And we all wanted ice cream.

Dad gave us some money and went back to his drinking. He truly believed we were going to the fruit market. And I know I didn't tell him about our plan to go to the petrol station.

We walked up the dirt driveway, out the gate and up along the dirt road. As I recall this, I can hear an ominous roar in my ears. Some of it is the noisy roar of peak-hour traffic, bumper-to-bumper on that highway just after five in the evening. But part of it is just that: an ominous roar. The soundtrack of my memory playing out like a horror film.

When we arrived at the highway, we stood on the edge of the traffic lane. Kevin was to the left of me, Ashlie on my right. It was 1984. There were no traffic lights. There was no pedestrian crossing. And we three children stood there for what seemed like hours, separated from the petrol station and the ice cream by a steady stream of cars. I can see a young boy's face through the rear window of one of the passing cars making a mean face at me as the car zoomed past. I remember wondering why he did that. He didn't even know me. I remember feeling hurt.

And after a while, I can remember Ashlie pleading with me, 'Jude, it's too busy. Let's go back.'

And I remember Kevin agreeing with her. 'It's too busy,' he said. 'Let's go back.'

And then, I can remember so clearly, I can hear my own little girl's voice in my ears, 'We'll be OK.'

And a break did come in the traffic, eventually. A little break, and I ran out first, across the lane of traffic approaching from our right. I got halfway, and made to cross all the way to the other side of the highway, but I saw that cars were still coming from our left, and I jumped back quickly to stand in the middle of the road, in between the lanes of traffic. None of us were holding hands, but Kevin followed my lead, crossing the lane of traffic from our right, striding out into the opposite lane but then seeing the oncoming cars, pulling back and joining me in the middle of the road. And Ashlie followed last. She crossed the lane of traffic approaching from the right, then blindly followed the both of us into the opposite lane. But it was too late for her to pull back and join Kevin and me in the middle of the road. A car collected her. I watched her body crumple like a rag doll across the car's bumper bar, the sound of screaming brakes and her legs, dragging along the bitumen.

I froze, a feeling of terror like ice water coursing through my veins. I turned to Kevin, screamed his name, but he was already turning around, running back towards the paddock. A woman got out of a car. She held me. She told me to look away. But I looked. I saw a group of men lift the front of the car off my little sister's broken body and I saw blood. And her sleeping face.

And someone asked a question, 'Is he OK?'

And I roared, 'SHE'S A GIRL! SHE'S A GIRL! THAT'S MY SISTER!' As if anyone could mistake her angelic face for a boy, even in those blue jeans and grubby shirt.

My dad arrived. He'd been drinking all day but he'd sobered up pretty fast. He yelled at me to get back to the house. He looked me square in the eyes and said, 'This is all your fault.'

And I know you're thinking I was just a child, I couldn't be held responsible for any of this, it was just a tragic, senseless accident. But he was right. No matter what way you look at it, it really was all my fault.

I turned and walked back to the house, a feeling in the pit of my stomach the likes of which I'd never known before now. My mind was on a loop, replaying the scene again and again, my little sister's limp, broken body wrapped around that bumper bar and dragging along the bitumen.

Carol was at the house when I arrived. She pumped me for answers. 'What happened? Was she awake when you left? Was she still alive? Was there lots of blood? Did she say anything? Did you see her move? Was she still alive?'

But before long I was unresponsive, almost catatonic, just shivering and gagging as if to vomit, and Carol put me in a bath. And I sat, rocking, in the bathtub, wondering where I was going to live after my parents kicked me out of the house. And out of the family.

And after a while, all Carol kept saying was, 'At least she's alive. At least she's alive.'

Somewhere there I ended up at Aunty Vera's house. Aunty Vera's was our second home when we were younger, and it wasn't far away from Charlie's paddock. I was in the lounge room, I remember, with Aunty Vera and my cousins, when Mum arrived, hours later.

She opened the door, her face changed, the features rearranged in an expression of grief that never quite smoothed over, even now. She looked at me and said, 'She's gone.'

Ashlie had survived the accident for a time, but she never regained consciousness. Every bone in her little body was smashed and her insides had been pummelled to a pulp. The decision was made to turn off the life support. If she had survived, my mother repeated a thousand times, she would have been a vegetable. And for months this was the mantra that we were all to repeat again and again, taking comfort from this tiny snatch of logic in a world of complete chaos.

It was a blessing that she died.

2

I see the days following Ashlie's death as if from the bottom of a pool. That sick feeling in my guts wouldn't shift, even though I felt relieved that it looked as though I was still allowed to live in the family home. I know I struggled to sleep and eat, as did my mother, who lost a dramatic amount of weight in the following weeks and months. I can remember that Anthony wasn't told that his sister was dead until the following day because the doctors advised letting him recover from surgery first. When Mum told him, he said very little. For some reason, he wanted to know whether the driver was drunk.

The morning after she died, Mum told me to jump over the back fence and tell the neighbour, Mary, what had happened. I wandered past their pool to the back door and knocked. Mary came out in her dressing gown and when I told her, she burst into tears and ran towards the fence, where Mum was standing. I can see Mum looking into Mary's face and sobbing, 'My baby! My baby!' and Mary cradling my mum's head against her chest across the top of the low fence and shaking her head in disbelief. Telling people was awful. The more people who knew what had happened, the more real it became.

Mum took comfort in the church. The priest, some nuns and her church friends filled the house, praying decades of the rosary around a statue of the Virgin Mary on the lounge room coffee table. There was a funeral to organise, hymns to select, a coffin to purchase. The house was full of the sickly scent of flowers sent by well-wishers who had no adequate words to express their heartfelt sympathy.

I had never been to a funeral before and had no idea what to expect. I certainly knew the inside of a church and could imagine that a funeral was just another variation of a regular mass. But my ten-year-old brain panicked every time the conversation turned to the 'burial'. Even though I didn't want to, I agreed to attend the funeral, but when it came to the burial, I was adamant I wouldn't be going. The priest and family friends urged Mum to talk me into it, for the sake of closure and acceptance. What none of the adults knew, and what I didn't think to explain to them, was that in my child's mind, the burial involved opening the coffin, lifting my baby sister's mangled frame out of the box and lowering her into the ground before throwing shovelfuls of dirt on top of her. I honestly had no idea that the actual coffin would also be buried with her. They were such beautiful and expensive pieces, I truly believed they were too good to bury, that they'd probably be reused. Eventually, I was persuaded to attend the burial as well, but right up until the point they lowered the coffin into the ground, I trembled with dread at the thought of seeing my sister's body. It was an almighty relief when the burial was over and it hadn't been what I was expecting.

Still, I was so lost. Ashlie had been my shadow, so when she was gone, I felt hollow. I remember kindly family friends taking me to their house and distracting me with cake making, games, craft and contrived conversation. I overheard whisperings about the psychological impact that witnessing my sister's death might have on me. And I learnt that grief and trauma did indeed do strange things to the mind. A couple of months after Ashlie's death, a cousin of mine had a birthday party, a fancy dress. Mum took me to a fancy-dress shop, where we both hired 'flapper' dresses, à la 1920s *Great Gatsby* style. I was thirsty and asked the shop assistant for a drink. But when she returned with a glass of water, for some reason I was convinced she was trying to poison me. Too ashamed to refuse the water for fear of being rude, I took a few small sips. I looked at the shop assistant, studying her face, convinced I could read her devious intentions. Within seconds, the poison was flooding my body. My face began to throb, my ears burned, my heart raced and legs buckled underneath me. The pounding in my ears reached such a volume I could barely hear myself when I turned to Mum and told her I'd been poisoned and she needed to take me to hospital, immediately. Mum was confused momentarily, but before long she was able to see this episode for what it was: a panic attack.

It was the first of many. It seemed I was always on the verge of death, usually by poison. A spider had bitten me, a meal had been laced with arsenic, I'd accidentally drunk petrol thinking it was red cordial. In fact, I remember Mum taking me to see a psychologist once or twice. I can remember a white-haired lady with a strange accent trying to make me re-enact the physical symptoms of a panic attack, encouraging me to take short, quick breaths to start hyperventilating. I was so severely self-conscious I clammed up, non-cooperative, and announced to my mum in the car after the session that the psychologist was the crazy one.

But I certainly wasn't the only one grappling with grief. They say that tragedy can either pull people together or tear them apart and it didn't take long for our little household to implode. In the initial months following Ashlie's death, I remember my parents displaying a tenderness towards each other that I'd never seen before. It was a shock, because most of my early memories are of Mum and Dad fighting; Mum yelling and Dad, drunk, laughing at her or ignoring her, joking about her behind her back to his mates. Mum has told me about Christmases she spent wrapping presents and trying to put bicycles together with Mamal, because Dad was nowhere around. But for a few months after the accident, there was no yelling. There was no fighting. It seemed neither of them had the energy for it. And for a brief time, Dad stopped drinking altogether. Everybody sort of floated through the house and around each other, learning, I suppose, to make room for what had happened.

But soon, all this floating put more and more distance between us, each player retreating to their corner to lick their wounds. Mum continued to work, traveling on the train from Penrith into North Sydney and back each day to her secretary job. Her mornings were early starts and she came home late in the evenings, often going to bed before the sun had set. I can remember her calling in sick to work sometimes and spending whole days in bed, pulling the blinds down and ordering everyone to keep quiet. She went to church, of course. Often.

I can remember that for a while there, Mamal lived with us, but by the time Ashlie died, she was in a nursing home. She had had a massive stroke a few years before, and the doctors said it was remarkable she even survived, much less learnt to walk and talk again. But she had dementia. She would ask us to help her to the toilet, then forget she had gone, and ask us again, every ten minutes, desperately scared she was about to wet herself. She had diabetes too and would beg us kids to sneak her sugary treats from the pantry when Mum wasn't around, which we would do, not really understanding how dangerous this could be for Mamal.

I remember it killed my mother to put Mamal in a nursing home. To make things worse, the only home she could get her into was halfway up the Blue Mountains, so Mum could only visit her mother on the weekends. Sometimes I would go with her, but the smell of old people and the depressing sight of twisted bodies moaning and dribbling underneath knitted blankets was too much for me. And despite spending so much time with her when I was little, it was hard to communicate with her. Poor Mamal had never mastered English and although I could understand her when she spoke to me in Latvian, I couldn't respond. It must have been a long, lonely week in between visits from Mum, without even being able to communicate with the nurses.

Early one morning, not long after Ashlie died, the phone rang. As soon as Mum answered, I knew the news. She quietly hung up, sat at the kitchen table and quietly cried. I learned later that Mamal had advanced breast cancer by the time she died. My mum suspected that the news of Ashlie's death might have triggered it. I've heard of that happening, and perhaps it was this that killed her, but at her age, it didn't seem to matter.

Dad never had a traditional job as far as I could tell. Mum tells me at one stage he had a lucrative truck driving company. We even took a family holiday overseas as a tax write-off. I can remember a couple of blissful weeks in Fiji, eating watermelon for breakfast, swimming in the ocean and making necklaces out of beads I collected on the beach. But by this time, Dad had lost his license too many times for drunk driving and it seemed that he surrounded himself with fair-weather friends; people who hit Dad up for money, then disappeared. Mum used to say he took little responsibility when it came to his own family but would give a complete stranger the shirt off his back. 'Your father always needs to look like the big man,' Mum would say. And despite giving up the grog for a short while after Ashlie died, I can only imagine the weight of the burden of guilt my dad carried. Not surprisingly, it didn't take long for him to find the bottle again.

One morning before going off to school, Dad gave me an exceptionally long hug goodbye. He told me that when I came home, he would be gone. He and Mum couldn't keep going and he was moving out. I went off to school sobbing uncontrollably and kept it up all day. My already tattered rug was being ripped clean from underneath me. I remember wandering over to Ashlie's old classroom and standing in the doorway, collapsing with tears so convulsive the teacher took me off to sickbay. And I remember there was no one they could call to come and pick me up.

My brother got on with school and his mates. He was in high school by then and I saw very little of him. At one point, our garage was converted to a bedroom, and Anthony spent his time out there, listening to Australian rock bands like Cold Chisel and Australian Crawl and smoking cigarettes and weed. I remember Mum being called up to the school to deal with a few of his physical altercations. As soon as he could, Anthony left school and took on an apprenticeship as a motor mechanic. He got his licence and bought a car, a red and black Torana, the first of a series of hotted-up cars he would own.

My mother and I began to fight with the fierceness of rival lionesses. We're close now, incredibly so, but I believe for many years she couldn't look past the fact that my actions had robbed her of her baby girl. And now that I'm a mother too, I do understand. She seemed to hate me, could barely stand the sight of me. She hated my friends, who never came to our house because my mother was so angry and rude to them, and to me right in front of them. I spent a lot of time alone in the house. When high school started, I would leave an empty house, take the long walk to the bus stop that took me to the Catholic girls' high school I attended and in the afternoon I caught the bus again, walking home to an empty house. Mum wouldn't arrive until hours later, usually exhausted and silent. Otherwise yelling at me for making a mess. Mum loved everything to be perfectly tidy. Friends and family often joked she had champagne taste on a beer budget. She would spend thousands on expensive furniture, couches she didn't want me sitting on, but I had holes in my school shoes and lived on toast and raw cookie dough. I can remember sit down family meals every night before Ashley died, but never afterwards.

Our tense relationship was only exacerbated by my closeness with Dad. I don't remember Anthony spending too much time with Dad, but Dad and I spent a lot of time together. He had moved out to a men's boarding home. He lived in a ramshackle house with four other men. The carpets were sticky, the coffee mugs were chipped and the whole house stank like washing that had been soaped up in the bathtub and strung across the back of the kitchen chairs and hadn't dried properly, because that's how they all did their washing. Most of them drank, heavily, and there were often fights. One of the boarders came after being released from prison, but within a few months he'd wound up back inside after holding up a service station with a loaded rifle. I remember Dad trying to explain to me that some people were actually happier to be in prison. It was my introduction to the concept of institutionalisation.

All in all, it was a pretty depressing place, but I'd sooner be there than home. And besides, I had a one-track mind: horses. I was absolutely horse mad, I always had been. Dad had a few paddocks he was leasing here and there, trying his hand at wheeling and dealing in cattle, sheep, anything that might earn him some coin. I was forever hearing his mates spout clichés like 'Your dad could sell sand to the Arabs, ice to the Eskimos!' He was definitely up to all sorts of no good as well. A bag of chequebooks and bank cards bounced around on the floor of his car, with a whole range of different names. Once, I answered the phone at his place. When he heard me tell the woman on the phone that no one by the name of John Crawford lived there, Dad leapt up and scrambled to the phone, quickly telling her there'd been a misunderstanding and he was, indeed, John Crawford.

But strange as all this was, Dad was also into horses and that suited me. He frequented livestock auctions and purchased any old nag going cheap, all of which I fell in love with, many of them uneducated under saddle and dangerous to ride. I had plenty of tumbles into barbed wire fences but nothing would scare me off horses. I was forever truanting from school and walking kilometres along the highway to Dad's place, begging him to take me riding. Or better yet, begging him to let me tag along to an auction to watch him bid on anything he thought might turn a profit: horses, cattle, sheep, goats. I even got a weekend job at some racing stables, working six a.m. to four p.m. every Saturday and Sunday, feeding yearlings and thoroughbreds in racing and mucking out stables, hard physical work, quite dangerous too, and measly pay at two dollars an hour, but I loved it. And I spent every cent of my hard-earned cash at the saddlery store; a new brush here, a bright red halter and lunging lead there. I always wanted to do the horse scene more seriously than Dad's budget or alcoholism would allow. I dreamt of pony club gymkhanas and shows, matching jeeps and gooseneck horse floats, shiny horses, gleaming tack, elegant riding jackets and ribbons braided into my horse's tail. I read horse magazines obsessively and knew all about every horse-related event for a hundred-kilometre radius. I filled out entry forms for various events and posted them off myself, begging Dad to take me. And he did sometimes. I can even remember him dropping me off at a showground the night before a show and me sleeping in the stable with my horse, Dad coming late the next afternoon to pick me up. I lived for this lifestyle, but looking back I was a pretty sad sight with my mismatched tack and novice riding skills atop of my uneducated rogues compared to the rich girls astride their handsome hacks.

There was also plenty of disappointment. Dad was good at making, and breaking, promises. I can think of countless times he promised to meet me at the paddock and take me off to a gymkhana and I would make the long walk from home out to the paddock, carrying tack and my grooming bag. I'd be there at the crack of dawn, washing my horse, doing my best to braid his tail and plait rosettes into his mane, painting his hooves and polishing my saddle. The morning would come, and go, with no sign of Dad. Eventually, I would grow tired of waiting and walk along the highway up to Dad's boarding house, usually to find him still in bed, sleeping off a hangover. A few times, there was even a strange woman in his bed, younger than him with long, brown hair hanging over the edge of his shitty little single mattress. I felt something close to hate then. My self-centred desires had no room for my poor, lonely father's quest for intimacy, no matter how temporary.

This pattern of broken promises and disappointments shaped my relationship with Dad as the years went on, but that did nothing to taint my deep love and affection for him. He was a happy-go-lucky character who always made people laugh, a hopeless, 'harmless' drunk. There were snatches of true bliss in my past with Dad. He loved telling me stories and teaching me sad, Irish ballads around the campfire. He was always so proud of my emerging guitar and songwriting skills, making me play in front of anyone who would listen. Wayward animals would make their way to him. He always had a loyal, mongrel dog at his heel. He loved practical jokes. He'd pick up hitchhikers in his VW and pretend the car had broken down and ask them to pop the bonnet, thinking it hilarious when they walked towards the wrong end of the vehicle. When I was older and living in the city, he'd make the trek out to Newtown to visit me. He'd take me to the pub and give his running commentary as the news bulletin played on the television, making me laugh with his conspiracy theories, and I'd joke that it took a dodgy man to spot a dodgy plan and he'd buy me a beer and even slip me a fifty if I was doing it tough.

Sadly, much of my fondness for Dad stemmed from pity. Photos of my father when he and my mother first met show a handsome man, well-dressed with immaculate hair and sparkling blue eyes. But the combination of grief and guilt and a lifelong battle with the bottle left him broken. He moved around from boarding houses to run-down flats and finally settled into a housing commission home in St Marys. He'd walk back and forth across the dimly lit park, riddled with whores and drug dealers, to drink at the St Marys Band Club, where he eventually died one afternoon, nursing a beer and waiting for the badge draw. He had hoarders' syndrome and after he died my brother and I cleaned out his house and it took three days and four skip bins. He had seven televisions and none of them worked. He'd bolted a security door lengthwise across his window and he slept with a hammer underneath the pillow and a knife beneath the bed.

He had a pet goose in the backyard named Gilbert. Dad was the only one who could get near him. If anyone else dared to approach him, the goose would shriek and gnash out savagely. After Dad died, Anthony wanted to take Gilbert to the RSPCA but I got all sentimental and insisted I'd look after him. And I took him home but the dogs got into him, breaking his wing and tearing a hole in his back and I sobbed and sobbed and begged my husband to take him out to his parent's farm and hit him on the head with a shovel.

Another living creature I'd taken responsibility for. And failed.

3

I got in with an odd crowd in high school; a bunch of misfits who didn't really belong anywhere else. We weren't pretty enough to be popular, skillful enough to be sporty or smart enough to be nerds. But we all had pretty quirky personalities that bounced off each other. We laughed a lot, and also got into a fair bit of trouble. Me, in particular. At an all-girls school, without the pressure of boys to impress, I embraced the role of class clown. I engaged in arrogant banter with my teachers, challenging them mercilessly in front of my peers to gain respect, or at least attention. Looking back on that time, I would like to apologise profusely to all my high school teachers for being the most obnoxious excuse for a student Caroline Chisholm High School has ever seen. And I would also like to assure them that now, having been a high school teacher for twenty years, I've definitely had more than my fair share of karmic retribution. And most importantly, I would also like to thank many of them, my English teachers especially, for seeing, and for nurturing, a light in me that spurred me into what has been an incredibly rewarding career.

But back to high school. One thing set me apart from my high school peers. I was the only one who had had a boyfriend. One night in Year 8 I attended a blue light disco, an iconic, alcohol-free, 80s dance party for under-eighteen moles and spunk-rats. Boys in pointy-toed shoes and stonewashed denim, girls in fluorescent socks, plastic sandals and absolutely enormous hair, doing the 'Nutbush', or later in the night if they were fortunate enough to 'get with' somebody, swaying arm in arm to Madonna's 'Crazy for You' while the smoke machine pumped carcinogenic smog around the PCYC Hall. I met a boy (let's say his name was Bradley), who gave me a love bite (a trophy sure to skyrocket my pulling power at school on Monday) and asked for my phone number. He rang the next day and so began my first serious relationship with a boy.

Bradley was too old for me. I was fourteen, he was seventeen. I was in junior high school, he had left school, had an apprenticeship and owned a car. He would pick me up on a Saturday night, but because I was way too young to even try passing myself off for eighteen, instead of hitting the pub or nightclub, we'd drive around in his panel van, doing laps of the main street listening to Billy Joel. Sometimes we'd go to McDonalds and meet up with some of his mates who also drove cars. We'd hang out in the car park, eat fries and drink shakes, AC/DC and Bon Jovi playing loudly from the stereo of somebody's car. Bradley would stand around cracking jokes with the boys, I stayed shyly in the background, the dutiful, demure girlfriend, looking on quietly from the bonnet of Bradley's car, grateful for every time he wandered over to put his arm around me or lay a 'pash' on my face.

But mostly, we went parking. Bradley would take me to a vacant block of land near the railway tracks and we'd smoke hash, get semi-naked and have awkward, uncomfortable sex that was usually interrupted by a spanner in my back or the thumping of a toolbox against my head. I don't remember ever enjoying these sessions. As Bradley's girlfriend, I was mostly terrified of an unwanted pregnancy, and Bradley, at least, was very mindful of that too. Each time he drove me home after one of our parking sessions, we'd stop at the football oval and Bradley would take our used condom and run it under the tap, filling it with water and holding it aloft to make sure there were no holes in it. It took me a long time to agree to go all the way with Bradley and it involved countless conversations, negotiations and flat-out threats from Bradley along the lines of 'If you don't put out soon, I'll find a more mature girlfriend who will.' He was also insanely jealous, often following the school bus to school, demanding that I come to his car before going through the school gates to kiss and fondle. About eight months down the track when I finally broke up with him, I was relieved to be free of his suffocating attention, and relieved also that, for the next few years at least, I was no longer sexually active.

Caroline Chisholm High School only went to Year 10. For Years 11 and 12, we moved on to McCarthy Senior High School in Emu Plains. The school was co-educational and was made up of the students from three main feeder schools; Caroline Chisholm all-girls school, St Dominics at Kingswood all-boys school and St Columbus school in the Blue Mountains. The students from St Columbus had been attending a co-educational school since Year 7 so it wasn't too much of a change for them, but for those of us who had been at a single-sex school for the last four years, it took some getting used to, and it definitely had a negative impact on my self-esteem and social skills. I was still interested in riding horses and generally taking centre stage as the class clown. Unfortunately, both these endeavours were deemed extremely uncool in front of boys. My peer group became more interested in hair and make-up and clothes and shoes and movies and music. I was gradually informed by my peer group that my nose was too big, my arse was too wide and my acne so appalling I should invest in Clearasil, concealer and foundation immediately! I was talked into more than one woeful haircut or new colour by my domineering 'friends'. I became self-conscious and anxious, retreating into a world of self-loathing. I couldn't maintain eye contact, my acne-scarred features squirming beneath the judgemental gaze of students and teachers alike. I dieted obsessively, skipping breakfast, taking no food to school and starving all day, only to stop at the milk bar on the way home to purchase, and devour, an entire packet of Tim Tams.

I was reasonably bright and able to skate along on natural ability in English at least, but I soon discovered that this approach wasn't going to cut it for the Higher School Certificate. If you kept skipping school to go horse riding or didn't do the recommended reading or keep up with your homework, it was extremely difficult to keep your grades up. In Year 12, I flunked my half-yearly exams. Suddenly my peer group buzzed with conversation about university acceptance scores, tertiary education and, gulp, careers! I was confronted with the daunting prospect of choosing 'something to do with my life'. I had no guidance from home whatsoever I vaguely remember Dad telling me I was too tall to be a jockey and that a hairdresser he knew seemed to 'do all right'. But my peers were putting in university applications and, for want of anything better to do, I took that path also.

And I'm so very grateful that I did. Between the half-yearly exams and the HSC trials, the lights seemed to come on. I knuckled down and improved my marks considerably, eventually scraping together a TER (Tertiary Entrance Rank) that was good enough to get me into university. The only problem was, I had no idea what I wanted to study. Somewhere along the line, I had gotten the impression that psychology sounded pretty cool, so I applied for, and was accepted into, a psychology course at Macquarie University, Ryde. But on the enrolment day, I made the huge trek from Penrith across to the university and everything about the day, and the uni, felt wrong. Firstly, I knew nobody else who had been accepted into Macquarie University, so I was all alone. I had no money, so moving out of home was not yet an option, and I couldn't imagine surviving the commute for the duration of my degree. And finally, and most importantly, the subject selections that made up the psychology course were predominantly science-based. I'd barely passed biology and knew that the course I'd selected was not for me. I decided to defer my studies and take some more time out to decide what I was going to do.

Getting a full-time job and earning some serious money seemed the next logical step. I threw a résumé together and hit the pavement, putting job applications in wherever I could. I had more work experience than the average teenager, having worked at the stables, then at a bakery and then waiting tables at Sizzler restaurant through my senior high school years. Eventually, I scored a job at a discount bookshop, which I was initially excited about, seeing as how reading was one of my favourite pastimes. The shop was in the city, so I joined the world of commuters, catching a bus to the railway station early in the morning, catching the train and then walking from Wynyard station to the bookshop up on Castlereagh Street each day. But the job was anything but glamorous. It was a dimly lit, poorly decorated store that stocked piles and piles of dusty, discount books. There was a major bus stop right outside the door and I would go home every night with a film of black grit on my skin and feeling as though I'd spent the day sucking on an exhaust pipe. My bosses were an elderly couple who would announce every few days that the War section suddenly needed relocating to the Cooking section and the Travel books ought to swap places with Kid's Picturebooks. I spent most of my time there loading my arms up with stacks of books and doing circuits of the store.

During the year, I still saw a fair bit of my schoolmates. We'd get together on weekends and hit the town. We loved dancing in nightclubs until the ugly lights came on at three in the morning, then heading off to a café to eat pizza or grab a kebab. We also loved watching live music. If one of us had a boyfriend with a car, we'd all pile in and head up Parramatta Road to the Annandale Hotel or the Landsdowne to drink beers and watch long-haired boys play electric guitars. Our 'look' had matured to reflect the early 90s grunge scene. It was cut-off shorts over nylon stockings, Doc Marten boots and blue-black hair. And it was on one of these nights out that I met Jimmy.

Jimmy happened to be the brother of a girl I'd worked with, but we didn't meet through her. My mates and I were at a local nightclub, drinking green-coloured cocktails and busting a move to MC Hammer's 'You Can't Touch This'. I found myself in a circle standing next to a tall guy who had soft features, beautiful hands and was wearing a Joy Division T-shirt. I later learnt he had a velvet speaking voice as well, but it was difficult to hear over the thump of the bass. We talked, or yelled, as best as the situation would allow, and he offered to buy me a drink. By the end of the night, we were holding hands and Jimmy took my phone number.

It turned out Jimmy worked in the city also and lived the life of Dr Jekyll and Mr Hyde. He had a fancy office job and wore a suit and tie by day, but at weekends he lived for sinking beers and watching live music. He loved music and had literally thousands of CDs. Together, we took in all manner of entertainment: Tori Amos at the Seymour Centre, Nirvana at the Coogee Bay Hotel, Iggy Pop at the Big Day Out. Jimmy would make me awesome mix tapes and he introduced me to literally hundreds of tracks that made up the soundtrack of my life; Mud Honey, Sonic Youth, the Cocteau Twins, Dinosaur Junior, Souxie and the Banshees, Throwing Muses, Club Hoy, Nick Cave, Leonard Cohen, Billy Bragg, Neil Young, the Sundays... I could go on.

For most of the year, Jimmy and I enjoyed a really beautiful relationship. We often caught the train to and from work together and would meet up in the city after work on Friday to drink cheap red wine and eat soup and garlic bread at a dingy jazz bar. I can remember what a consolation it was to meet up with Jimmy after another dull and dreary day stacking piles of books. My friends adored him. My mother even liked him. He was polite and intelligent and cool and he treated me well. And he was truly a romantic. I sent a box of nuts to his work with a little card inside: 'I'm nuts about you!' In return, he had a shoebox couriered to my work. Inside was one of his shoes with a pebble glued to the inner sole and a note – 'Girl I love you so much/That baby it's such/I'd walk a mile with a stone in my shoe – from Billy Bragg's 'The Price I Pay'. He even took me down to Melbourne for a weekend for my birthday, treating me to a fancy hotel and *Phantom of the Opera*.

Despite this joyful relationship, other areas of my life were nosediving. By the end of the year, I found myself unemployed. I had been sacked from the bookshop for reading all the time. (I actually thought it was good product endorsement but the bosses walked in one day and told me they could have walked away with half the store and I wouldn't have noticed.) So my boyfriend had a degree and a bourgeoning career in finance, my friends had a year of university under their belt and I seemed to be staring down the barrel of more mind-numbing retail. I decided that since I loved reading so much, I might as well enrol in uni and put my passion to good use.

4

I do know that I decided studying literature was probably a logical trajectory for the immediate future, but I honestly can't remember ever decidedly choosing teaching. I honestly seem to have just fallen into it, perhaps because the double degree of a Bachelor of Arts/Bachelor of Education at Newcastle University was the only course that I was remotely interested in and also eligible for. And by now, I'd managed to save a little bit of money, and moving out of the house and away from my mother looked incredibly appealing.

So I was nineteen, and about to learn a harsh lesson about the vast chasm between expectation and actualisation. I sent off my university enrolment paperwork and began fantasising about my brand-new life. It was so tangible, so palpable. I was finally going to be a grown-up. I would be studying at uni and I was going to be living with intellectuals who would also be studying at uni. We were all going to sit around our beautiful little share house with its mismatched furniture and Frida Kahlo prints, cooking vegetarian casseroles, drinking red wine and smoking Drum tobacco. We'd share poetry and philosophy and there'd be men with long hair and goatees and Blundstone boots who would fall desperately in love with me. A whiteboard and marker would sit by our front door, inviting our myriad visitors to leave a message if they dropped round and we were all out, presumably visiting other unimaginably cool and bohemian share houses.

These were the thoughts I entertained myself with as I rode the Sydney–Newcastle train line in search of my new digs. This was the ideal I visualised as I circled advertisements in the share house accommodation classifieds, feeding twenty-cent pieces into a public phone, pounding the pavement between trendy addresses, sitting through interviews at kitchen tables with leaseholders who reigned supreme, like monarchs in castles.

I went from share house interview to share house interview. Unfortunately, so did hundreds of other university students chasing the same accommodation arrangements as me. For every spare room, there seemed to be a dozen of us standing in line. My desire for a spacious bedroom with a balcony overlooking the ocean was scaled down to a smaller bedroom with an en suite, then recalibrated to a dingy bedroom at the end of a hall until eventually a broom cupboard looked inviting. I even applied for a share house that offered a room that wasn't even a room at all, but was actually half of the lounge room, separated by a bedsheet tacked to the ceiling.

And still, none of them wanted me and each rejection spun me into a deeper pit of despair. For a time, it looked as though I would be sleeping at the caravan park, but I finally found a room in an ex-Baptist church. My cousin helped me move, hitching a box trailer to the back of his car and loading up my clothes, some books and a double mattress. My mum was home when we drove off, standing out the front watering her camellias, and I don't remember her asking me for my new address.

If you're picturing an ex-church with high ceilings and wooden floorboards, leadlight windows and the scent of residual frankincense, that is, university digs jackpot, think again. It was literally on the wrong side of the tracks and was both literally and metaphorically miles away from any of the addresses I'd inspected. It was neither near the uni nor the beach. To get there, one needed to catch a train to Hamilton station, alight and turn in the direction of Islington, then walk past a motley crew of street walkers; bikies, drug dealers and ladies of the night, to get to the building, which had all the character of a run-down community hall. It stank; a disgusting, cheap dishwashing liquid smell. The 'bedrooms' had once been confessional boxes and mine had black, circular smears all over one wall where the other occupants had been playing squash. The tiny window was at least nine feet above the floor and was covered in vines, so the room was in a perpetual state of dusk. I would wake to mice running across my doona.

The flatmates weren't funky, red wine-quaffing, Nick Cave-listening, art house-film aficionados. In the rooms on either side of me lived 'Surfers for Jesus' (because, let's face it, that's exactly what Jesus would want us to do). They held regular prayer group meetings and on the rare occasions their doors were ajar, I spied realms of biblical passages scrawled all over the walls.

In another room dwelled a mousy junky. He was invariably clad in black Levis and one of his AC/DC shirts and the only thing that could coax him from his room where he sat playing with Star Wars figures was the news that his dealer was at the door. He told me that a really cool party had been held at our place once. In keeping with the church theme, invites came dressed as their favourite Bible character and a swimming pool was created in the immersing bath beneath the floor in our lounge room. But I saw no such thing.

In the coveted front room lived the leaseholder and one of the most enigmatic characters I've ever met. She was a buxom, middle-aged woman studying medicine and I was perplexed at her willingness to reside in such a dump. She'd speak longingly about her husband and family back in Sydney in one breath and in the next, would relay frighteningly graphic stories of her sexual encounters with various men at her work.

Other 'flatmates' came and went, but they moved on as soon as they found a better arrangement, which wasn't hard. The bathroom was just a tiled room with a laundry tub and a showerhead sticking out from a wall. The kitchen was just a sink and a couple of hotplates. I don't even think we had a fridge and we definitely didn't have a television. I spent nights in my room drinking beer, smoking cigarettes and listening to the Indigo Girls on my Walkman. And I studied. For this first year of university at least, I studied hard, not because I was hell bent on blitzing my course but because I believed that I was so stupid there was no way I was going to pass uni. I was certain I would flunk and be kicked out and then Lord knows what I was going to do. So I did the long bike ride out to the uni campus and back every day, always racing to get home before dark because I lived in terror of someone knocking me off my bike and stealing it, such was the calibre of characters in our neighbourhood. And I went to lectures, and I attended tutorials and I studied hard. And in that first year I earned some pretty decent marks.

But this did little to lift my spirits. A darkness settled over me that I was to become all too familiar with. Jimmy was still in Sydney and I missed him, horrendously. I would catch the train down every Friday night to meet up with him in the city, where we'd drink at a bar before catching the ferry back to his share house in Mosman. The upper-class suburb he had moved to spoke volumes about the growing fissure between us. The weekends became less and less enjoyable for both of us. I was horribly depressed, drinking heavily and crying constantly. I'd gained weight, living on beer and cheap, crap takeaway, and I wore op shop rags that took my grunge look to the next level; ragged cheesecloth skirts, stained, suede jackets and oversized work boots. My eyes were lined with heavy-handed kohl and I sported studded dog collars around my neck. My fingers were stained nicotine yellow and my hair always stunk of a rank mix of patchouli and drum tobacco.

Eventually, Jimmy told me to meet him on a street around the corner from his work rather than come into the office. He didn't want any of his workmates seeing his grubby girlfriend. Every Sunday evening, he'd see me off at the station as I caught the last train to Newcastle, back to my mouldy mattress on the floor of my putrid little room. Invariably, tears would be streaming down my face and sometimes I sobbed so hysterically Jimmy would warn me to pull myself together and stop embarrassing him.

Jimmy suggested I try making friends. He knew a couple of old school friends who had gone to Newcastle uni and had chosen to stay on in Newcastle and find employment there after they graduated. He put me in touch with a married couple, Lara and Paul. Lara invited me to come along to an indoor netball game and enjoy a bit of 'hit and giggle' with the girls. I hadn't touched a netball since Year 2, where I spent a season playing goalkeeper because I was freakishly tall and couldn't catch, or shoot, a ball. But hey, why not? I thought. She seemed totally unperturbed by my confession of having zero netball skills and made it sound like more of a social gathering.

She picked me up and drove me to the indoor netball centre, introducing me to the team. I was mildly alarmed at how trim and fit they all looked. I was pretty certain none of them spent most nights smoking rollies, sinking long necks and listening to the Indigo Girls. They put a bib on me, something about 'winging defence' or something. 'Don't worry, you'll be fine,' Lara assured me. 'Just have fun.'

And then the whistle blew. A gathering of relaxed young women turned into feeding time at the zoo. Girls were zipping around the court, screaming instructions at each other, their frantic voices barely audible over the squeak of their sneakers twisting on the court. Girls were shoulder barging each other, thrusting their arms out in front of each other, kicking and tripping each other, their energetic dance carried out to the tune of the umpire's whistle. I had absolutely no idea what was going on. The few times the ball was actually thrown my way, I dropped it or received a shrill whistle followed by an announcement from the umpire: 'STEP! HELD BALL! OFFSIDE!' Jesus, I thought, she sounded like an SS guard. I'd stand there like an idiot until a decidedly pissed-off player gave me a pathetic look and snatched the ball from me. After the first quarter, I had bruises coming out on my forearms and a concerned member of the opposing team asked me how long I'd suffered from asthma. It was suggested that I sit the rest of the game out and, needless to say, Lara and her netball team never asked me back.

Jimmy suggested making friends with some of the people in my uni course. I guess I could make small talk with some of them, but for the most part, I was the proverbial black sheep. Most of them took their studies very seriously and many talked about the importance of excellent results leading to becoming a 'targeted grad'. They wore the sensible clothes of, well, teachers, and I never ran into any of them at the uni bar at lunch. There were quite a few mature-aged students among them as well. These were the most intimidating, with their life experiences of travel, families and alternative careers. I just didn't fit in.

At one stage one of the girls hosted a party. She lived at home with her family in a respectable suburban home, and in the backyard was arranged a big circle of plastic chairs around tables laden with nibbles. I was much more interested in the bathtub full of chilled wine and ciders and proceeded to get completely sloshed, getting louder and, I imagine, more obnoxious with each passing hour. I remember feeling unwell at one point and took myself out to the front yard for a break and what I suspected would soon be a spew. But when I turned the corner, I stumbled upon a couple of guys from the course sharing an enormous spliff. They offered me a toke. I'd had a bit of a poorly hidden crush on one of these guys for a while. Not wanting to look like a wuss in front of them, I accepted the roach and sucked it down hard. Before too long, I remembered the jingle, 'Grass then beer, you're in the clear. Beer then grass, you're on your arse.' I knew things were about to get really messy.

I have massive blackouts from that night. I have no idea how I managed to collect my things and get myself to the train station, but I wound up alone on a train to Sydney that arrived at about three o'clock in the morning. I can remember vomiting on the train, moving away from the vomit to another seat to vomit some more, getting off the train to join a connecting train and vomiting on the platform, then passing out on the second train. When I knocked on Jimmy's door before the sun came up and he saw the state of me, he was furious, lecturing me on the dangers of binge drinking, travelling on trains alone in the middle of the night and generally being a complete dickhead. I scoffed at his reprimand and told him to chill out, but of course, he was right.

Things at the share house ex-church got even worse. I came home from Sydney one weekend to find that the lock on my bedroom door had been smashed and my room had been ransacked. The violation was devastating. I didn't own anything of particular monetary value, but they stole things of untold meaning to me; my little stereo and my CD collection, clothes and shoes, university textbooks and assignments, the precious mix tapes Jimmy had made for me. To rub additional salt into the wounds, what they didn't steal they smashed. My lamp was in broken shards all over the floor, my clothes horse was in fractured pieces. And worst of all, my main form of transport, my pushbike, was gone.

All my flatmates feigned complete ignorance as to who the culprit might have been. It seemed suspicious to me that entry to the house hadn't been forced, only the lock on my bedroom door had been broken. One of the Jesus surfers eventually told me that although he didn't have actual proof, I should start by looking at one of the tenants in the front room, a young girl who we suspected was doing heroin who had a bogan boyfriend who always wore a cowboy hat and was definitely doing heroin. The surfer admitted he had seen a pushbike that looked a lot like my pushbike in her boyfriend's backyard. Whether any of this was true, I'll never know, and it didn't matter. Although the police came and took a statement, I never saw any of my stolen goods again, but in their wisdom, the police thought to interview aforementioned junkie flatmates and tell them I suspected they were involved. My flatmate and her boyfriend arrived at the front door one afternoon with a group of tattooed thugs brandishing baseball bats and threatening to shut me up permanently if I went to the police again.

A few weeks later, I came home from uni one afternoon to find my other junkie flatmate, the one who played with Star Wars figures all day, scratching himself like a mangy dog. He stood in the hallway and lifted up his shirt to reveal a torso riddled with raised, red lumps. 'It would seem we have lice,' he announced. When I mentioned that perhaps we should seek out the landlord for a resolution, he told me, 'Yeah, about that. We're not actually on a lease.'

'So, the money I put into an account every fortnight, where does that go?' I wanted to know.

Junkie Star Wars fan shrugged, scratched at his bitten tummy and wandered back into his room.

I decided it was probably time to move out.

5

I haven't said much about my mother in this story so far, and what I have said hasn't painted her in a glowing light. But this has to be said for Tina: there were plenty of times when I really needed her, and she came through with the goods. No sooner had I hung up the phone after telling her about the robbery, the threats and the lice than she was in her car and headed up the Pacific Highway to collect me and my measly pile of remaining belongings.

Together, Mum and I rocked up at Jimmy's front door. By this time, Jimmy had moved out of his share house in Mosman. He and a mate of his had shifted into a three-bedroom terrace house in Surrey Hills. It was on Smith Street, not too far a walk from Central Station. I managed to talk Jimmy into letting me have the third bedroom, which was a small, cold hovel, with pavers for flooring and a wall of glass doors that opened out to the even smaller back courtyard; a jungle of overgrown weeds and a wood paling fence that looked like a strong gust of wind might blow it over. I don't think Jimmy or his mate were mad about the idea of me moving in, but it reduced their share of the rent, and it was probably pretty hard to say no to the sight of a desperate, sobbing girlfriend and her black garbage bag full of (probably lice-infested) clothes, especially in front of her fretful mother.

I still had about half of second semester of first year left. It's unfathomable to me now, but I actually commuted from Sydney to Newcastle to attend lectures and sit my final exams. Don't ask me how I managed it. Where there's a will, there's a way! But even before the end of the uni year I had firmly made up by mind. By hook or by crook, I was getting out of Newcastle, for good.

It was brought to my attention that, provided one's grades were good enough, it was actually possible to transfer to another university. This was news to me but something I began investigating immediately. I sought out the relevant people, filled out the relevant paperwork and was told that I would be notified by mail if my application for transfer was successful.

In the meantime, I set about forging a new direction. I'm sure that even on my teaching salary I couldn't afford to pay the rent on an inner-city terrace today, but this was almost thirty years ago, and even a grungy uni student relying on Austudy like me could afford to pay the rent. Just. But if I wanted to eat, or more importantly, buy tobacco and drink at the pub, I needed to find some work.

Once again, I was pounding the pavement armed with my résumé. I can't tell you how many unpaid trial shifts I did, only to learn that this was a sneaky way some pubs, bars, cafés and restaurants got free help. Trial shifts were almost always given on a Friday or Saturday night when establishments were packed. You'd waitress your arse off, giving them your best performance and go home without so much as a cut of the tips, only to not hear from them again. I finally ended up with a part-time gig back at Sizzler in Bondi Junction, the same franchise I'd worked in at school. Hourly rates were pretty crummy but if they employed you part-time, you were guaranteed a certain number of hours per week.

I actually really enjoyed working at Sizzler. I was a hard worker and knew the ropes backwards. Workmates would specifically request to open or close with me because they knew I'd do most of the work. I made some really good friends there, many of them backpackers who were out for a good time. The end of each shift was usually celebrated with a drinking session at one of the many pubs in the junction, or if we were really planning to go off, we'd all squeeze into a cab and go down to one of the bars on the beach. Once again, I don't think I could afford a piss-up at the Bondi Hotel these days, but this was more than thirty years ago, and there were plenty of dives with cheap beer, juke boxes and pool tables.

For a time, Jimmy and I enjoyed the novelty of living together. Even though I had my own room and I was working shift work, mostly at night, which meant Jimmy and I were working very different hours, we had some really nice times, cooking fettuccine carbonara together, sharing a bottle of wine and snuggling up on the couch to watch Hal Hartley or Quentin Tarantino movies. Jimmy had a stereo, his thousands of CDs stacked up in boxes that were strewn around his room. We'd go to bed, holding each other to the swooning tunes of the Sundays or Neil Young. Sometimes we'd take a walk up Pitt Street, browsing through second-hand bookshops and second-hand CD shops, eventually making our way to Circular Quay, where we'd sit on the pier, eat ice cream and watch the lights of the ferries coming in from Manly.

But time was running out for me and Jimmy. Where Jimmy felt comfort in the routine and security of our de facto arrangement, I felt shackled. Through work, I was making new connections with people my own age. I'd work late, party even later and spend the morning in bed while Jimmy went off to work. Jimmy could sense me slipping away, chasing I don't know what. Adventure. Unpredictability. Chaos. I was uprooted, content to throw care to the wind and see where it took me. We started fighting, savagely. He hated my smoking, my filthy ashtrays stinking up the bottom floor of the house. He hated my drinking and stumbling in the door at all hours. He suspected, correctly, that I'd started dabbling in drugs and, most of all, he hated the dismissive way I shrugged off his criticisms. Sometimes we'd scream at each other for hours, our arguments swirling and threading in a coil so tight they choked us. We were over, and I needed to move out.

Once again, I found myself at the kitchen table, pen poised over the share accommodation classifieds. I inspected rooms in Dulwich Hill, Paddington, and every suburb in between. One evening, I rang a number for a room in Surry Hills and spoke to a chirpy, friendly girl named Julie. We chatted easily, but when she gave me the address, I gasped in disbelief. It was on the same street as Jimmy's terrace, just across the road and a little way down the same block. Initially, I thought it was pointless to even consider moving somewhere so close to Jimmy, but when I visited the house and met Julie and the other flatmate, Karen, everything clicked into place. They offered me a beer and the three of us sat around the kitchen table, smoking cigarettes and chatting easily about who we were and what we liked to do. No sooner had I returned home than they rang and told me I had the room. Not long after I moved in, I received some more good news. My application to study a Bachelor of Arts/Bachelor of Education at the University of New South Wales had been successful! I need never go anywhere near Newcastle again.

The terrace was tiny. Julie and Karen took the two bedrooms upstairs, I had the front room downstairs, which was actually a partitioned section of the living area. The wall dividing my room from the lounge room didn't even go all the way to the ceiling. There was absolutely no front yard to speak of whatsoever. The front door literally opened up on to the street. As I lay in bed, pedestrians and cars passed by my front window merely a couple of metres away from my head. Similarly, anyone coming through the front door was only a metre away from my bed. The lounge room had no windows and nobody had a TV. We didn't really have a proper lounge either. We all lay about on beanbags, drinking beers, smoking cigarettes and listening to music. Julie was a chef, so she did similar hours to me. Karen had a proper office job at a bank in the city, but that didn't stop her joining in on our frequent drinking sessions.

In the day, we spent most of our time sitting at the little table in the little kitchen, which was a tiled room with a little window next to the little sink. Julie would serve up Danish pastries and make us all stovetop coffee, served in wide bowls without handles, telling us 'That's how they do it in Paris.' She'd sip at her coffee, a pastry in one hand, a lit cigarette in the other.

Unbelievably, the combined toilet and bathroom was right next to the kitchen. You could be sitting at the kitchen table and lean across without getting out of your chair to open the sliding door and see the toilet. There was no laundry, but we did have a washing machine. The girls had it on hire and just included the rental fee in the house rent. The washing machine was in the tiny courtyard out the backdoor, the electrical cord fed through the bars on the bathroom window and plugged in above the bathroom sink. When the sun was shining, we often sat in the courtyard. It wasn't actually big enough for any outdoor furniture, even if we had any, but we sat in a circle on upside-down milk crates, the hard surfaces making criss-crossed patterns on our backsides.

Despite getting along well with the girls, the fact was, they were a fair bit older than me. I was twenty, they were closer to Jimmy's age, and there was never any question about who the leaseholders were and who called the shots in our house. When they'd had enough and wanted to go to bed, I had to call it a night, even if I wasn't ready for it. If they were awake but I was still in bed, there was never any attempt made to keep the noise down and let me sleep. They weren't backwards in coming forward, often telling me it was my turn to fill the food pantry or buy the next pack of toilet paper or case of beer, which was problematic because I didn't earn anywhere near as much as they did and had a hard time keeping up with the expense of Julie's preferred brand of coffee and all of the hard drinking that we did.

I can recall one story that best demonstrates this imbalance of power in the Smith Street household dynamics. Early one morning, I woke to my alarm. I had an opening shift at Sizzler and needed to get across to Bondi by nine a.m. I entered the bathroom and turned the shower on. Just then, Julie knocked on the bathroom door. 'Jude, can I just use the toilet before you have a shower?' I turned the shower off, wrapped a towel around me and stepped out of the bathroom so that she could use the toilet. But after a minute or two, I heard the shower start up and saw plumes of steam creeping through the bathroom door. To make matters worse, her boyfriend soon descended the staircase, opened the bathroom door and joined her in the shower. I stood in the kitchen, shivering, wrapped in my flimsy towel. By the time they finished with the bathroom, I didn't have enough time for a shower, and doubtless they had used up all the hot water anyway. I went upstairs and donned my uniform, spraying my pits with deodorant and doing my best to tidy my hair. I headed off to work without a word of complaint to Julie.

Another story comes to mind when I recall Julie's reign supreme. I remember once I was walking home from the bus stop after work. I passed a stray dog, a collarless black and tan kelpie with a friendly face. It was most unusual to see a dog, a typically working dog breed at that, wandering aimlessly not far from busy Oxford Street. I bent down to pat his head and resumed walking, the friendly kelpie close at my heels. By the time I got home, he was still right beside me. I fetched my house key out of my bag and he stood there patiently waiting for me to open the door as though we did this daily. I opened the door and he followed me in.

The girls weren't home. I gave the dog some water and scrounged around for something I could give him to eat. He took a long drink and then curled himself up at my feet. When I got up to get myself a beer from the fridge, he followed me across the kitchen and back again. To anyone looking on, it would seem this dog had been my faithful companion since his puppy days.

I was immediately smitten by this dog's sweet and loyal demeanour. I couldn't begin to imagine where he had come from but he certainly didn't appear to be fretting for his owner. It truly felt as though he'd been sitting there waiting for me to come along. I knew I would have to make some attempt to locate his owner, which would consist of placing 'Lost and Found' posters around the neighbourhood and calling the council and the local vets, but I was already expecting that no one would claim him and I was already fantasising about the joyful relationship between me and my new canine companion. Yes, we had a ridiculously small backyard that was completely unsuited to even a small dog, much less a kelpie capable of running a daily marathon, but I was an energetic, active girl who had no car and walked absolutely everywhere. I'd even be able to ride my bike with my dog running alongside me I reasoned. By the end of my first beer, I had named him: Beau.

Beau and I snuggled up on a beanbag together in the lounge room, me drinking a stubby, tickling his chin and massaging his ears, Beau tilting his head and virtually moaning in ecstasy. And that's how Julie found us when she walked through the door.

'What's all this about?' she asked.

'Julie,' I beamed, 'meet Beau.'

Beau smiled up at Julie sweetly, already seeming to respond to his new name.

'And who does Beau belong to?' she wanted to know.

'Well,' I ventured, 'maybe, now, us.'

'Ah…no,' she quipped with firm finality. 'No, no, no, no!'

Julie moved behind Beau, nudging him with her steel-capped toe all the way to the front door. She pushed him out on to the street, slamming the door behind him.

'But,' I protested, 'you can't just throw him out onto the street!'

'Well,' Julie retorted, 'where did you find him?'

Of course, she had me there and I had no response. All I could do was sit and listen to Beau's gut-wrenching howls from the other side of the front door.

'Don't you dare go out there, Jude!' Julie warned from the kitchen with all the severity of an irate mother. 'He'll move on,' she assured me.

While Julie twisted the top off a beer, I peeked outside my bedroom window. Beau was standing there gazing mournfully at the door. My heart was aching and tears welled in my eyes.

Of course, Julie was right. It was preposterous for me to even entertain the notion that I was in a position to become a dog owner, but still, she'd been completely brutal. But as Julie predicted, Beau did eventually move on. And that was that. As quickly as he had come into my life, Beau left it again. But I've never forgotten my brief yet poignant relationship with that beautiful dog.

There's another story from my time living with Julie and Karen that, in hindsight, is much more humorous but was no less stressful at the time. I'd been doing an afternoon shift at Sizzler. A new guy named

Mal had been doing his first trial shift in hot side, seasoning steaks and flipping patties. We'd been chatting breezily and both of us sensed more than a bit of chemistry. When my shift came to an end, Mal asked me whether I'd like to meet up for a drink later. I agreed and we arranged to meet at the Lizard Lounge up on Oxford Street at seven p.m.

I headed home, buzzing from the flirtatious afternoon and the prospect of a potentially romantic evening. At about six o'clock, I decided it was time to have a shower. I flicked the kettle on, planning to have a cup of tea when I got out of the shower. This is a curious detail. Ordinarily, I would be slugging on a beer or sipping on a wine while I was getting ready to go out, but for whatever reason, on this particular day I was after a tea. So with kettle starting to boil, I stripped and turned the shower on.

Just as I was about to get into the shower, I noticed that my towel wasn't in the bathroom. In those days, I only had one towel, which was either wrapped around me, strewn across the bed or drying on the line. I quickly ducked out into the backyard, and just as I realised my towel was not, in fact, on the line, the backdoor slammed behind me.

For a few slow seconds, my mind could not compute what had just happened. Surely I wasn't locked out of my house without a stitch of clothing on?

And then the kettle started wailing.

Of course, it was one of those kettles that didn't automatically turn itself off. The gravity of my situation was crushing. Fortunately, the walls of our courtyard were enormously tall, at least nine feet high, so at least people who were passing by on the street couldn't see me. The same couldn't be said for the people who lived in the high-rise apartments that surrounded the house in every direction, but I just decided I wouldn't look up.

I reasoned that I had more than one pressing problem in need of a solution, so in a bid to gain some control of the situation, I began to prioritise. Firstly, I needed something that offered more covering than my birthday suit. You might remember I told you earlier that we didn't have a laundry. Instead, we had a washing machine in the backyard, just outside the bathroom window. I uttered a silent prayer and opened the machine to find (oh joy!) a wet load of Karen's washing. Of course, Karen was a good two sizes smaller than me, but you would be surprised how possible it is to squeeze a size fourteen arse into a pair of size ten shorts when your only other option is being naked in public. I found a teeny wet T-shirt to match that barely covered my torso, but at least now I wouldn't be arrested for indecent exposure.

Next, with the kettle screaming, I reasoned that I had to get the power off. I opened the back gate and padded around the front of the house looking for a power box. I found it, opened it up and turned every switch to the off position. It worked. After a moment, the kettle sighed and turned silent. The shower continued to stream water but I knew there was nothing I could do about that until I had access back inside the house.

In order to do that, I needed a key and the only key I had was on the wrong side of the door. The only other keys I could get belonged to my flatmates, who were both at work. Karen worked in the CBD. Julie worked at the Paddington Inn, all the way up Oxford Street. Julie was closer, and wandering along the street barefoot in wet, ill-fitting clothes was probably marginally less conspicuous on Oxford Street.

I headed up to the Paddington Inn and asked for Julie. I thought she might be furious that I'd embarrassed her in front of her workmates, but she found the sight of me, and the story that went with it, hilarious. She gave me the key, even offering me a cold drink and a cigarette. I returned home and had what was now a cold shower.

I even managed to make it to the Lizard Lounge in time for my date and I had an ice-breaking story to tell. And in case you're wondering… no, he wasn't worth it.

After about twelve months of living with Julie and Karen at Smith Street, the winds of change blew around. The girls had found a trendier, more expensive terrace uptown in Paddington. Of course, I was most welcome to move on with them, they told me, but the rent was more than double what we were paying for the shoebox on Smith Street.

Moving on with them wasn't an option for me and they knew it. There was a silver lining. I was still able to stay at Smith Street. The lease would be handed over to me and I was able to move into the main bedroom upstairs.

For the first time ever, I was to become the powerful leaseholder who would decide who could and couldn't move into my little house.

6

It turned out that being the powerful leaseholder hosting interviews to find a couple of new flatmates wasn't as good as I thought it was going to be. I let scary stranger after scary stranger into my house. There was the tattooed bikie who wanted to know if he could park his Harley in the hallway. There was the perfectly groomed beauty consultant who couldn't possibly live in a house with such a small bathroom. There was a retail worker who had two cockatoos in an enormous cage. And there was the gay yoga instructor who, without asking, opened my fridge, appraising, critically I imagine, the contents.

Eventually, I settled on a couple of backpackers, an Irish girl named Siobhan and an English girl named Joanne. The downside was that, being backpackers, neither had any cool furniture to contribute to the household. On the upside, they also smoked cigarettes, so they didn't mind me smoking. And they could really hold their drink.

I continued with my university studies and actually really enjoyed the Arts component of the course. I went to lectures on literature and engaged in tutorial discussions on everything from Shakespeare to performance poetry. I was also studying History and really enjoyed the lectures on Ancient History in particular, but I didn't feel as confident in my ability in History. Interestingly, my History marks were better than my English marks, probably because I made more of an effort due to my lack of confidence. But overall, I never topped the marks that I got in first year when I was studying at Newcastle. Now that I had a transfer and was living in Sydney, I relaxed and was quite content with passes and credits.

Something else I developed an interest in around this time was travel. A few people I'd met at uni had relayed their travel stories to me and I decided it was something I wanted to do for myself. One girl intrigued me with her stories of travel by bus around Indonesia. Another shared amazing stories of her island-hopping in Greece. Of course, living with a couple of backpackers from Ireland and England also piqued my interest in these far-off places. So between my Austudy and my waitressing wages, I tucked a little bit of money away until eventually I had enough for a return plane ticket to London.

I wasn't quite twenty-one when I did this trip. It was uni holidays, between semesters, so it was European summer. Back in those days, nobody had the internet to arrange their own travel plans. I remember the excitement of sitting in the travel agency and listening to the woman on the telephone reserving plane tickets and arranging transfers for me. I also remember my poor mother almost having a heart attack when I rang her to inform her that I was taking off for the other side of the world. I can still see her, almost in tears, taking a photo of me out the front of my house in Smith Street before she drove me to the airport. I'm wearing black jeans and boots, my henna curls hanging loose, my red and grey backpack perched on my shoulders, face full of excited anticipation.

I flew with Singapore Airlines and the travel agent talked me into making a stopover in Singapore on my way to London. I can remember the shock I felt to see such a military presence at Changi airport. Soldiers with huge guns swinging from their belts and German shepherd dogs on leads. I also remember wondering what I was supposed to do with the hole in the ground when I went into the ladies' bathroom. Where on earth was the toilet?

The travel agent had arranged transfers, so after I collected my luggage, a minibus took me to my hotel. It was so clean and there was an enormous queen-sized bed with crisp, white sheets. I remember taking a swim in the rooftop pool and lying on a banana lounge while a gentleman in smart black pants brought me drinks. It was such luxury, the likes of which I'd never known. I felt like royalty.

The next day, I got back on the plane and flew to London. The thrill of being at Heathrow airport, riding the 'tube', listening to people speaking with British accents, it was just amazing. The travel agent had suggested I stay at Earl's Court because apparently there were plenty of Aussies there. (The Brits called it Kangaroo Court, she told me.) I had organised some accommodation at the youth hostel. I hopped off the tube at Earl's Court and with my map sprawled in front of me, found my way to the hostel, stopping at every street corner to reorient myself. I can remember dumping my bag and heading off to sightsee immediately, soaking up the sights and sounds and smells of London for the very first time. The black taxicabs driving on the wrong side of the road, the red telephone boxes, some of them harbouring piles of human faeces from homeless people using them as a toilet, Hyde Park, Big Ben, Westminster Abbey, the Thames, the Tower of London. I'd never been to the city before in my life but having seen so many of these sights on the television, it felt like I had. I fell in love with London, and still maintain there's no other city like it in the world.

At the hostel, I slept in a dormitory-style room with a dozen other travellers. This made getting any sleep pretty difficult, with people coming and going and making noise at all hours, rifling through bags, chatting on their beds or snoring loudly. But it did make it easy to strike up conversations and meet people. I quickly befriended a girl named Nicola. Ironically, Nicola lived in Surry Hills, Sydney, Australia, within short walking distance of my house in Smith Street. We bonded over our hostel provided breakfast of lukewarm tea and marmalade on toast and made some joint plans.

I hadn't come to London with any firm plans other than to walk around a bit, see some sights and hop back on a plane bound for Sydney a month later. But Nicola had a working visa, so she was planning to squeeze in as much travel and sightseeing as she could before finding some work. She suggested we get on a bus and head for Manchester. Manchester! Home of some of the greatest pop music in the world! I'd heard so much about it and was definitely keen to join her.

My sincere apologies to anyone reading this who hails from Manchester, but back then in the 90s, it was a serious disappointment. The skies seemed to be permanently painted grey. The buildings were drab. People looked depressed, and knowing now what I know about the plight of the working class in the city at the time, it's little wonder. I remember Nicola and I went into a bottle shop to buy a bottle of wine to take with us to an Indian restaurant where we were planning to have a curry. The alcohol and the shop attendant were separated from us by sheets of bulletproof glass. We ordered the wine from afar, popping our money in a chute, after which the shop attendant dropped through our bottle of wine. It was pretty confronting for this twenty-year-old Aussie girl.

We even did some clubbing. I thought perhaps getting a taste of the underground party scene would bring some colour to the city for me, but it wasn't to be. Perhaps Nicola and I just didn't know the best places to go.

We hung around for a few days, then hopped back on the bus and made our way to Edinburgh. Now there was a city that exceeded all my expectations. The minute we stepped off the bus, we were confronted with the sight of a castle. A real castle! We shrugged on our backpacks and instantly set about taking each other's photo in front of this glorious scene.

We had pre-booked a couple of beds at a youth hostel. According to Nicola's Lonely Planet guide, the hostel was a mere '5 m' away from the bus stop. So we started walking. And walking. And walking. Five minutes came and went. Ten minutes. Twenty minutes. Half an hour. After an hour, we realised that five minutes didn't actually stand for five minutes. It meant five miles!

We had an absolute ball in Edinburgh. We loved the city, strolling along the streets, enjoying a pint in a bunch of pubs with names like the Black Bull and the Hanging Bat. We chatted with locals and at night, we crawled pubs. I had been studying conversational Spanish at uni and tried it out with a beautiful Spanish man named Jose. We ended up kissing but, to be honest, I don't think he understood a word I said.

After Edinburgh, Nicola wanted to stay up north and explore the Lake District. I decided that, as a Murphy, I couldn't come all this way and not visit Ireland, so we exchanged details and went our separate ways. I got on a bus and went back down to London and then flew across to Dublin.

My first thought about Ireland as the plane began to descend was, 'No wonder they call it the emerald isle.' In fact, as the lush, green coastline came into view, there was a collective 'oooohhah' from everyone on the plane, its beauty was so astonishing. I was so surprised to note how close Dublin was to London yet how different everything felt. The beautiful accents, the cobbled streets and styles of homes, the pubs. People were so friendly, it was impossible to sit quietly in a pub and have a beer without someone coming up and starting a conversation. I did find myself asking people to repeat themselves a lot. With such thick accents and speaking so fast, it was difficult to always understand what people were saying. But I just adored it. I caught a bus down to County Cork for a couple of days as well, which was also gorgeous.

After Dublin, I flew back to London and, with deep regret, caught my return flight home to Sydney. I would have loved to be following in Nicola's footsteps, finding some work, earning some money and doing more travel. But I had a room in a house in Smith Street I was still paying rent on. I had a university degree to finish. And plenty more adventures, both good and bad, still awaited me in Australia.

7

Not long after returning home from the UK, I had my twenty-first birthday. My mum went to great lengths to make this an enjoyable occasion. She had some landscaping done in the backyard at her house in Penrith and invited family and friends to sit around the pool, listening to music and eating sausages with pasta salad. I really was grateful to my mum, she had the best intentions, but my memories of the night are really quite sad. I was in a dark mood, feeling very lost and disconnected. Instead of socialising politely and responding graciously to toasts made in my honour, I threw back beer after beer, getting absolutely legless and sulking quietly in a corner.

To make it worse, Jimmy had been invited. The family had always liked him, and it's true we had managed to keep things civil between us since our split, but that night, the sight of him made me miserable. He reminded me of all my failings, all the opportunities for happiness that I'd managed to sabotage.

Back in Surry Hills, my backpacking flatmates had moved on and I was once again on the hunt for a couple of new tenants to help with the rent. I wound up living with two new girls who turned out to be my favourite flatmates ever.

Freya was a nurse. She was originally from New Zealand. I hadn't really met any Kiwis before Freya and I was always entertained by her unusual accent. She had red hair and pale skin and was forever lecturing me about the importance of wearing sunscreen and lifting heavy objects properly so as not to hurt my back. She often did stints of night shift and we'd wake in the morning to find her drinking a longneck and smoking a cigarette in the back courtyard at eight o'clock in the morning. Of course, she was simply winding down the same way we did after a shift, but it was always an odd sight, the three of us sitting on our upturned milk crates, us with our coffees, her with her beer.

Freya moved in first, but I needed another flatmate for the third room. I put an advertisement in the paper, and usually one would be inundated with people trying to find themselves a room to let, but for some reason, the only person to express any interest was a girl named Tash.

My immediate impression of Tash was a definite no. She had pasty white skin, stringy hair, dark circles under her eyes and she was heroin skinny. She spoke slowly. She blinked slowly. She moved slowly. I thought she could be trouble and I wasn't keen to have her. But like I said, she was the only person to show up for an interview, so I gave her the room.

It turned out I was wrong about Tash. She was definitely stoned the day she came to inspect the flat but she didn't do harder drugs. Well, no more often than me anyway. And the reason she was so stick skinny was because she'd not long broken up with a boyfriend and had taken it really badly. Tash turned out to be a lot of fun. In fact, the three of us lived together for almost two years and we had a really good time together. We were a regular trio at the Royal Albert Hotel, which was just at the end of our street. We'd sink beers, play pool and pump coins into the jukebox, singing loudly into the end of our pool cues to Tash's favourite song by the Murmurs: '...now there's dust on my guitar you fuck...'

After our drinking sessions at the pub, we'd bring home some takeaways and keep the party going in the back courtyard. Our neighbours must have absolutely hated us. I can even remember a couple of nights, a man in his pyjamas pounding on the back fence and telling us to pack it in. In which case, we'd take it into the house and turn the stereo on, dancing around on the lounge room floor and taking turns to climb up on the coffee table and sing into a hairbrush.

I remember after one of these partying sessions we finally called it a night and hit the sack. A few hours later, I got up to get a glass of water and found Freya, completely naked, passed out on the floor at the bottom of the stairs. I kind of shook her, tapping her face to try and rouse her until eventually she half came to and I dragged her up the stairs and put her back into bed. In the morning, Tash and I woke to find Freya gone. There was a message on the answering machine telling us she'd woken up in a lot of pain, unable to move her arm. She had taken herself up to the hospital to get it X-rayed and discovered she'd broken it in three places. Turns out she had got up to go to the bathroom but in her dazed state she'd mistakenly thought she was still living in her old house, the one that didn't have a staircase just outside her bedroom door. She'd missed the first step and tumbled all the way to the bottom of the stairs. After that, 'Judestar the Beer Monster' was also the girl that put her flatmate to bed with a broken arm.

There was also the night I came home from a drinking session with my workmates and the girls were already in bed. I had the munchies and was in the kitchen searching for a snack. I decided it would be a good idea to butter up some Saladas and put them in the toaster. (Yes, the best ideas always come to me when I'm drunk.) So I put the buttered Saladas in the toaster and then went over to the sink to fill the kettle. I spied, through the kitchen window, some flames across the street. Panicking, I flew through the front door, ready to pound on the neighbours' door and alert them to the fact that their house was on fire. But when I went out on the street, the house was fine. The flames had disappeared. I took my drunken self back inside and resumed filling the kettle but once again, through the window, I saw the house across the street on fire. For a second time, I raced out onto the street, but alas, the flames were gone. It took the third time of looking through the window for me to realise that the flames I was seeing were actually a reflection in the window glass. The toaster had set the Saladas on fire.

I remember around this time, cycling along Anzac Parade in Kensington on my way home from uni one day, I spied a guitar in the window of a music store. It was a second-hand Yamaha with a price tag of two hundred and fifty dollars. That was an awful lot of money for me back then, probably more than three weeks' rent. But I felt a new urge pulling at me. I wanted that guitar. Sure enough, I squirrelled some money away and eventually brought that Yamaha home.

I can remember that afternoon, squealing with excitement, lifting it out of its cardboard box to suitable 'oohs' and 'aahs' from Freya and Tash.

'That's great Jude,' Freya told me, 'but can you play?'

'Well, not yet,' I replied confidently.

The truth was I had held a guitar before. At school, in music class, we'd been taught a few basic campfire chords, and with some practice I was soon switching from D to A and back to D, then breaking it up with an E. I didn't really know any songs, though, so before too long I was seeking out some lessons.

My very first guitar teacher gave lessons in a little studio above the music shop where I'd bought my guitar. I bought a soft guitar case and strapped it over my shoulder, riding my bike out along Anzac Parade, feeling uber cool with my instrument on my back. I don't remember the teacher's name. I'm going to say John but I could be totally making that up. Anyway, Johns approach was to get me to bring in a song I liked. He'd pop it into the cassette player or the CD player and we'd listen to the song with him stopping and starting it, then writing down on a sheet of paper what the chords were. I learnt very little from this process other than that John seemed to be a musical genius and working out the chords to songs I liked seemed to me impossibly difficult. But I'd take the sheets home with John's mad scribblings all over them and pretty soon I was playing along to the Indigo Girls' 'Land of Canon' and Edie Brickel's 'Circle'.

The thing was, I loved to sing, so I was learning the chords pretty quickly to the songs I wanted to sing. And Tash loved to sing too. And so began a beautiful connection between the two us. We'd drink beer, light candles and have huge jam sessions, harmonising and singing along to Lisa Loeb, Tracey Chapman and Four Non-blondes. We both liked the old stuff too. John Denver, Olivia Newton-John and Patsy Cline. I'm not sure the neighbours thought it was quite as beautiful as we did.

One night the three of us were out watching a band at The Houpton Hotel. Towards the end of the night when we'd all had a few and the band was wrapping up, Tash asked the guy on stage whether I could borrow his guitar and get up and play a song. He said he was fine with it.

I was horrified. I couldn't possibly get up on stage in front of everybody! But Tash and Freya wouldn't let up. 'Judestar! Judestar! Judestar!' they chanted, physically pushing me up on the stage. And so while the band dismantled drum kits and unplugged leads, I sat on a stool with a guitar in my lap and a microphone in my face and sang, 'Me, I'm a part of your circle of friends, and we, notice you don't come around…' I was so insanely nervous my leg trembled, wobbling involuntarily as I tried to balance the guitar on my knee. I sang most of the song with my eyes closed, too afraid to look out at the crowd, but when I peeked I saw Freya and Tash, singing along with me and cheering me on. When I finished, the crowd clapped and whistled and called out, 'More! More!' And it felt incredible. I fell in love with that feeling. For the first time in my life, I felt like I was doing something that showed the world who I really was.

One day, a friend of Tash's told me I should sing at Brackets and Jam. I had no idea what she was talking about.

'Brackets and Jam,' she repeated, nodding enthusiastically. 'It's an open mic event at the Good Bar up on Oxford Street. I think it's on a Monday.'

Even the concept of an open mic event was new to me. Was this girl telling me you could go to pubs and bars where they just let anyone up on the mic to sing and all you had to do was put your name down? It turns out that's exactly what she was telling me, and I became a regular at Brackets and Jam. The event was run by a lovely guy named Clyde, a leathery hippy with beaded dreadlocks. Sometimes I'd play, sometimes I'd just watch, eating a space cake, drinking some chai tea and lounging back on a beanbag while aspiring musos played. Sometimes I wouldn't plan to play but someone would loan you their guitar and up you went. Everyone was so supportive and encouraging. It was a beautiful vibe. And at the Good Bar is where I met Mark.

Mark, or Marky as everyone called him, played guitar in a heavy metal band with a name that made absolutely no sense at all. They got up and played towards the end of the night. They were completely awful, the singer screaming incomprehensible lyrics into the mic, but I was immediately attracted to the guitarist's bad boy look: long dark hair hanging loosely over his dark eyes and goatee, black jeans, black T-shirt, black boots. After Brackets and Jam wrapped up, most people headed upstairs, where there was a square bar in the middle of the room surrounded by hundreds of people who were drumming on bongos and dancing. On the dance floor, Marky and I gravitated towards each other and danced and drank for hours. He walked me home. Well, I let him walk me as far as Crown Street. I didn't want him knowing where I lived in case he was actually an axe-murderer. I don't think we even kissed, but he gave me his number. He told me later he was sure I wouldn't call. But I did.

Marky lived near Bondi Beach and I went to visit him the next day. We went out for lunch and coffee and things took off pretty quickly. Marky was a really nice guy; it was hard not to like him. He had a simple mind and a good heart and he was completely smitten with me, always thinking about me, bringing flowers when he picked me up, driving me to and from work. But Marky had a penchant for mind-altering substances. He had friends with names like Benzo Benny and Tripper Pete. Marky loved nothing more than getting out of it, big time. He really introduced me to a whole new scene. Alcohol had always been my poison. I was a pub goer through and through. Tash and Freya hadn't nicknamed me Judestar the Beer Monster for nothing. But with Marky it was nightclubs, parties and bushland raves, eeing, speeding, tripping or coking, whatever we could get our hands on. We did some pretty crazy stuff, stripping naked and swimming in Bondi Beach at six in the morning. I'm still surprised none of the morning runners called the police on us.

But not long after I met Marky, something started happening to my body that kept me from keeping up with the wild parties (which, in hindsight, is probably a really good thing). One day after going to the toilet, I noticed that the toilet bowl was spattered with bright pink blood. I ignored it for a while but after a couple of times I got pretty concerned. I was also feeling really unwell, nauseous and dizzy, with excruciating stomach cramps. Sometimes I had little control over my bowels, barely making it to the toilet in time, and some days I needed to go half a dozen times within a couple of hours. I felt feverish and tired, my body aching with fatigue. The symptoms grew worse and were really starting to interfere with my life. Drinking alcohol would temporarily relieve the pain, not to mention the anxiety associated with it, but it would make me worse in the long run.

Freya was a nurse, so one day I opened up to her, asking her what I should do. Not surprisingly, her advice was to see a doctor immediately.

What followed was a series of humiliating conversations and examinations with doctors and specialists. I was asked everything from how often I went, when I went, what it looked like, what it felt like… I was subjected to pokes and prods in my stomach and my rectum, I was sedated and cameras were sent up my arse and down my throat (hopefully not in that order!) And it turned out I was diagnosed with ulcerative colitis.

It's very strange, being diagnosed with an illness you've never heard of, but it wasn't to be the last time it would happen to me. It's also very strange to be diagnosed with an illness you can't see, but unfortunately, it wouldn't be the last time that would happen to me either. But take it from me, colitis is absolute misery. Essentially, like Crohn's disease or diverticulitis, it's an autoimmune disease. The job of the body's immune system is to attack foreign bodies to keep you well. When you have an autoimmune disease, the immune system is confused and starts attacking healthy things in the body, for instance, the lining of your bowel. Left untreated, the bowel can perforate, in which case, you're completely fucked. The way colitis is treated is with immunosuppressants; drugs that, as the name suggests, suppress the immune system so that it stops attacking healthy parts of the body. The downside, of course, is that you're immune-compromised. Much of the medication is trial and error. What works for someone might not work for another, and if you can't get on top of it, doctors may prescribe steroids.

The next decade of my life was overshadowed by the stormy clouds of ulcerative colitis. I endured one hospital admission after another, unable to tolerate food or fluids, placed on drips and mega doses of hydrocortisone, or steroids. And everything they say about 'roid rage' is absolutely true. These drugs drove me completely mental. My face blew up like a balloon, I gained weight without eating anything, I cried, I was uncooperative and non-compliant, screaming at the doctors, the nurses, my mother, blaming anybody I could think of for the hell that was this horrible disease.

The negative impact on my mental health couldn't be overestimated. At one point, even though my physical health was temporarily stable, I was exhausted and depressed. I was more than halfway through my uni degree by then, but I needed some time out. I had finally let the lease go on my little house on Smith Street. Freya had moved in with a boyfriend over on Bondi Beach and Tash had moved in with a good friend across the other side of Surry Hills. I had been living in Newtown for a while with a gay couple, having met one of them through my new job at a hotel up on Crown Street. But I decided to defer my studies, put my measly belongings in my mum's garage and head north. Everyone was raving about Byron Bay, full of whale-watching tree-hugging hippy-healing. That's where I'd go to get over this horrible illness. I'd meditate and walk along the beach and get off the grog for good.

Mum was visiting a friend in Queensland anyway, so she drove me up there. She told me later that when she dropped me off in downtown Byron Bay with my backpack and guitar, she cried all the way back to Sydney. And there was plenty to cry about. I didn't find fame or spiritual fortune in Byron Bay. It turns out when you run away, your problems run after you. I had no luck getting off the grog, every man and his dog had a guitar and I don't remember seeing a single whale.

No matter, I thought. I'll go even further north. Nicola, the girl I had met when I was in London, was back in Australia. She was up in Port Douglas, working at a hotel there. I'd go visit her. It took two full days on a Greyhound bus but I made it to Port Douglas and tracked down Nicola. She had a spare room and was happy for me to move in and help with the rent. But things didn't work out like I'd hoped. Nicola had a boyfriend, a new hairstyle and sensible shoes. She was studying hotel management, was planning a wedding and saving for a sports car. Whatever we'd had on the other side of the world was long gone. And it didn't matter anyway. Within a week, I was admitted to Port Douglas Hospital, my bowel haemorrhaging and stomach twisted inside out. After a week on a drip, I was back on a Greyhound bus headed home to Sydney, collapsing in my mother's arms when she met me at the Central Station bus stop.

8

I wish I could say the years I spent in the grip of colitis were the darkest days of my life. I had no idea the troubles that were brewing on my horizon, and of course, it's just as well.

After coming home from my disastrous 'journey of healing', I spent a couple of months with my mum. I had to visit the hospital every couple of days for check-ups, removing my pants, rolling onto my side and bringing my knees up under my chin, often unable to answer the doctor's questions through my tears of humiliation and despair.

My weight was impossible to keep down due to the huge amounts of steroids being pumped into my body and my mental health became just as precarious as my physical health. I can picture me sitting for hours at my mother's kitchen table, crying, or just staring into space. Mum suggested getting in touch with my school friends or visiting members of the extended family (namely my beloved Aunty Vera) but I flatly refused. I wouldn't even answer the phone; not that anyone called for me anyway. I didn't want to read, or watch TV, or play my guitar. I did go for walks, often for hours, walking down to the Nepean River and sitting under a tree, my Walkman playing Tori Amos's 'Little Earthquakes' in my ears.

My mum worked at the hospital by now, as an assistant to a professor of haemoglobin, so she had a lot of medical connections. She arranged for me to see a psychologist. Unsurprisingly, I was diagnosed with depression and placed on antidepressants.

Despite being chronically ill, I can remember feeling like a complete failure having moved back home with my mum. Of course, she wouldn't listen to me talk that way, and she made it clear that I was welcome to stay there as long as I liked, but the weight of my unfinished uni degree hung heavily on my shoulders. Before too long, I found myself some work in a café and spent a few weeks on a mate's couch before finding a room in a share house in Newtown. It was on Church Street, not far from the famous cemetery. When I moved in, there was an enormous hole in the kitchen floor. You had to walk around it to turn the stove on and you could see all the way through to the dirt beneath the house. It seriously took months to get the real estate to fix that hole. I can remember we'd come home from the pub on cold winter nights and pin beach towels across the kitchen door, turn the gas oven on and sit around it with the door open, smoking cigarettes and trying to keep warm.

Once again, I was living with a mixed bag. Santos was the lease holder. He worked at the same café I worked at. That's how I found the room. He was a gay beach bum, a gentle, hippy character who woke us up at six o'clock every morning with the grinding of his blender making a wheatgrass smoothie.

James took the front room, which was the best and most expensive room in the house, with a balcony overlooking Church Street. He had long hair and glasses that made him look like John Denver. I never saw him without his black pork pie hat on. I'm certain he slept in it. He worked in film and television and was forever bringing good-looking, well-dressed people into the house. The manner in which he introduced them to me indicated that they were halfway to being famous and I should be suitably impressed, but I'd lived in share houses without a television for the past four years and I didn't know who any of them were.

In the front room downstairs lived Maree. She was the youngest one in the house. She was studying make-up artistry, not just glamour make-up (which she was absolutely brilliant at) but special effects, zombie-apocalypse-movie style make-up. Like me, Maree loved to drink and loved to sing, often at the same time, and we listened to a lot of music together and had a few singalongs. She was a beautiful-looking woman with an extraordinary figure, acutely aware of the sexual power she wielded over men. She brought plenty of them home. (I have an excruciating memory of accidentally walking in on her giving some guy a blow job.) But Maree mistook sex for love and she was always confused and disappointed when the men she brought home didn't stick around. I don't mean to sound condescending here. It took me years to learn this harsh lesson: that just because a man wants to sleep with you it doesn't mean he likes you. Just because a man hangs out with you for a few weeks, it doesn't mean his head won't just as easily be turned by another. I was a very slow learner and have plenty of anguish-ridden song lyrics to prove it.

I have an anecdote about one of these hard-learned lessons from around this time. His name was Michael Hanrahan (not his real name, of course, but his real name did have the same perfect two-syllable first name, three-syllable surname rhythm). We'd locked eyes one night across the smoky room of Taylor Square's the Judgement Bar. He sidled up beside me as the Cranberries blared in the background. We swapped 'digits' and it turned out he was also at UNSW.

For a couple of weeks we 'dated', meeting up for lunch in the quad, laughing at people having what we called 'Christian sex' on the library lawn, discussing David Lynch and proposing ridiculous and pretentious theories about Erasurehead. He would surprise me by showing up at my work, watching me pull beers till I knocked off, then taking me out drinking till the early hours, when we'd find some park swings and watch the sun come up, smoking rollies and singing Billy Bragg. I dragged my poor flatmates across the inner city to watch his awful, awful metal band (what was it with me and metal heads?) swooning at his long hair and silver spandex pants, fantasising about his fingers playing me the way he played that cheap, bass guitar.

Imagine my elation, then, when he greeted me at the door one afternoon, face beaming with childish exhilaration, telling me he had tickets to the *Star Wars: The Phantom Menace* premiere. My mind was a herd of runaway horses. Where would we be sitting? What would I wear? Who would I ask to cover my shift? And then the effort it took to remain composed and look completely unaffected when he said, 'So, I've decided, with this hair and all, I'm going as Princess Leah. Would it be OK if I borrowed that long, white dress of yours?'

Of course, I gave him the dress. To refuse him the dress would be admitting that I cared, but after seeing him out I slid down the door, a gloom settling over me as dark, I imagine, as the one that clouded over George Lucas after those terrible reviews were released. He did, at least, return the dress, albeit covered in lipstick and cigarette burns.

Anyway, having re-enrolled in uni, I dug in, determined to finish my teaching degree. There was a significant practical component to my teaching degree and I spent the good part of a term as a prac teacher at James Cook Boys Technology High School at Kogarah. My supervising teacher, Steve, is one of the many, many amazing people I've had the good fortune of meeting throughout my career. He was extremely supportive, he had such a great sense of humour, excellent rapport with the students and he even brought his dog to school on occasion. I also experienced one of the funniest moments in my teaching career during this prac.

James Cook Boys had a high population of Greek and Macedonian students. In my Year 9 English class there were many big, burly boys who were pretty loud and unruly. Then there was Ronnie. Ronnie was Asian, a softly spoken, graceful student with exceptionally manicured hands. The footy lads gave Ronnie one hell of a hard time, mimicking his accent and constantly calling him 'poofter'. Of course, I would reprimand the boys, warning them with detentions and behaviour monitoring cards, but this did little to curb their enthusiasm for mercilessly taunting poor Ronnie. Ronnie, to his credit, remained composed, quietly getting on with his work, but his English was poor, and Ronnie didn't understand the connotation of this word, 'poofter', that the boys directed at him. But one day it must have got the better of him and Ronnie did some investigation. A little way into the lesson when one of the jocks in the back row dropped the term 'poofter', Ronnie stood up and addressed the class, very clearly and confidently, 'I am not poofter! But if I was poofter…I would not fuck…any one of you!' I could barely contain my laughter and I beamed at Ronnie with pride. I didn't hear any of the boys taunt him again.

Life rolled on and between my prac, my studies, my work at the café and then my job pulling beers at the Rose of Australia Hotel in Erskineville, it's hard to fathom I had any time for socialising. Colitis was still regularly rearing its ugly head. I can remember checking myself out of hospital to put in a shift at the Rose of Australia so that I could pay my rent, pulling beers with my hospital name bracelet still wrapped around my wrist, then checking myself back into hospital. I was on a first-name basis with the staff at St Vincent's and things got so bad that surgeons even began discussing the possibility of me needing a colostomy bag. I recall having a heated conversation with a nurse, me telling her I'd sooner be dead than shit in a bag, her telling me (rightly so) my attitude was rooted and I should be grateful for the medical assistance available to me. But somehow I managed to squeeze in a relationship with a man named Chris.

It was the early hours of the morning and I was sinking beers at the Oxford (my home-away-from-home during my years in Newtown). Chris was just my type. Long hair, dark features, black jeans and boots, chain-smoking Dr Pat tobacco. He was a brooder, very quiet, content to sit and listen, tugging at his cigarette. We liked the same music, read the same books, watched the same films, he even wrote poetry! I fell for Chris in a huge way, and we had some really romantic times. We'd hold hands on the couch, eating his homemade lasagne, quaffing red wine and cracking up at Paul McDermott on *Good News Week*. On the weekends we'd sleep late, then go up to the 'Erko', where they served all-day breakfast, and we'd order bacon and scrambled eggs, smoke cigarettes, drink the first beer of the day and read the paper. We even travelled to Byron Bay together and I was always so grateful to Chris for helping me repair my feelings about the place after my earlier experiences. I was never much into footy but Chris was a big AFL fan, and he introduced me to the excitement and atmosphere of a live game. And let's face it, any activity that let me drink beers in the day was going to win me over. We were both there, cheering wildly, when Plugger kicked 1300.

I met his family and they adored me, especially his mum, who was a teacher. She placed a lot of pressure on Chris to get more serious about our relationship. But Chris never felt the same way about me. My ongoing health issues, physically and mentally, put a cracking strain on our relationship and after about eighteen months we parted ways.

I took the break-up with Chris really hard. It had been clear from the start that I was never going to be the love of his life and the failure of the relationship solidified an already significant conviction in me that I was unworthy of love. That I was unlovable. My alcoholism escalated (if that can be believed) and I went through a sad time of promiscuity, desperately searching for love, or simply attention, from anyone willing to give it. I was the subject of the Indigo Girls' 'Blood and Fire' – 'I am intense…'

I had a few other issues that caused me a great deal of grief around the time Chris and I broke up. On top of my usual colitis-related hospital admissions, I was admitted to hospital with pneumonia. I'd been ill with a flu I just couldn't shake and by the time I needed to be admitted to hospital, drawing breath was like being whacked in the chest with a cricket bat. Initially, they suspected meningitis and I was placed in an isolated room, hospital staff not daring to come anywhere near me unless it was absolutely necessary. Eventually, they diagnosed pneumonia and they placed me in a ward for more than a week. When I moved out of Church Street, I discovered that the underside of my futon mattress was dotted with mould, which could go some way to explaining that. I also had my wisdom teeth out, all four of them, under anaesthetic. To rehash the sporting equipment imagery, I looked like I'd been smashed in the face with a baseball bat for a good two weeks. My cheeks were so swollen I could barely move my tongue to speak.

I'd also been asked to leave the Church Street house. Santos had an enormous falling out with one of the other flatmates. When I defended the other flatmate, I lost my room too.

At this point, I wasn't up to finding another share house. I didn't have the energy to try and sell myself to another leaseholder and navigate my way through another complex share house group dynamic. I decided to go for a lease on a one-bedroom place and live alone. Of course, this was going to be a lot more expensive than a room in a share house. In Newtown, the further away from King Street you lived, the cheaper the rent. I found myself a place so far away from King Street I was actually a couple of suburbs away in St Peters.

It was a tiny terrace, jammed in amongst a row of tiny terraces. There was a little front gate with a small, concrete slab out the front, where I'd sit in the morning sun with a coffee and a cigarette, reading the serial numbers on the bottoms of the planes that flew overhead, so low and loud that if you were speaking on the phone when one flew over, you'd have to hang up and ring back. The terrace opened up to a long hallway. The tiny bedroom was off to the right, then the hallway opened up to a small living room. You walked through that to get into the kitchen and then the bathroom at the back of the house. The backdoor opened up to a small yard that previous tenants had actually put some effort into. There were raised garden beds along the fence line with lavender and roses and bulbs popping up all over the place. It was all very 70s; wood panelling on the walls and pink tiles in the bathroom, and there was a most unpleasant smell to the place that no amount of air freshener could eradicate, but it was all mine.

My mum came to visit, kindly bringing me some pots and pans and kitchen utensils. (I still have a Tupperware strainer she gave me all those years ago. I'm sure it would survive being run over by a truck.) I remember how nice it was to make my mum a cup of tea in my own place, drinking out of my own cups, sitting in my own living room. And now that I had no flatmates to answer to, I decided it was high time I treated myself to what had been a long-held desire. I was going to get a dog.

Mum could see how important this was to me, and she could also see the merits of me having some canine company now that I was living on my own. Mum drove me out to the RSPCA at Yagoona and together we went looking for what was to become my next big love.

It was really difficult, looking at hundreds of sad puppy eyes and wanting to take them all home, and initially I wasn't sure I could choose any of them. But then Mum pointed out a puppy with long legs and pointy ears. She looked like a German shepherd with perhaps a hint of Kelpie. She was the one. We drove home with me cuddling and bonding with my new best friend the whole way. A sweet face like hers deserved a sweet name, and I called her Hannah.

Hannah turned out to be a super intelligent dog. Within days, I had taught her to sit, stay and come when I called her. She was easy to manage on the lead and she followed me everywhere. Eventually, I only had to think a command and Hannah would do it. I've had a few dogs since Hannah and I've adored all of them, but I know I'll never have another dog like her.

So it seemed that things were coming together for me at last. I had finally finished my uni degree, having sat my interview with the department and earned my certificate to start teaching. It was with great delight that I resigned from my pub job. I vowed that I would never work another Christmas Eve, Christmas Day, Boxing Day, New Year's Eve, New Year's Day, Easter weekend, Anzac Day or any other public holiday ever again! (Of course, I have actually done some school work on these days over the past twenty years, but officially, I haven't had to 'go in' to work.) I was getting quite a bit of work casual teaching at James Cook, where I'd done my prac, as well as Glebe High School.

My mum was making some pretty big changes in her life as well. She had retired from her job at the hospital and had sold her house in Penrith. We had a cousin on the Gold Coast that Mum was close to and, a few years earlier, my brother had gone up there and found some work as a motor mechanic. Now Queensland was calling my mum, who bought a cute little house at Mudgeeraba. She helped me settle in to my digs at St Peters, then with an emotional goodbye on my front door step, she got in her car and started the drive up north to her new home.

It was literally a few hours after Mum left, I was sitting in the sun tickling Hannah's ears when the phone rang. An official-sounding voice asked to speak with Judith Murphy.

'Speaking,' I replied.

'Judith, this is Wendy Parker calling from the Department of Education Human Resources office. I'm ringing to offer you a permanent teaching position at Quandialla Central School.'

9

'Where the hell is Quandialla?' were the first words to pop out of my mouth.

Wendy explained to me that it was a small country town in the central west, some hundred kilometres the other side of Cowra.

'Well, I don't even have a car,' I told her stupidly.

'Hhhhmmm...' she mused. 'Well,' clickety click of her computer keyboard, 'according to my computer, there's a train line that runs through Quandialla, so you should be fine.'

My poor mother. She was only a few hours up the road. She had called in to visit a friend on the central coast to break up the trip and fortunately, I had her friend's number. I caught her there and told her what had just happened.

'Where the hell is Quandialla?' was the first thing she said.

My mum turned round and came back down the highway. She spent the night with me and the next day she drove me to Quandialla and back. We left early in the morning, crossing the Blue Mountains, going through Bathurst, Cowra, Grenfell, and finally, around six hours later, we sailed into Quandialla.

The first thing we did was laugh our heads off at Wendy's comment about a 'train line' running through Quandialla. After a little sign alerts you that you've arrived in town, you cross a single train track that disappears into wheat-coloured paddocks in either direction. Mountainous silos stand like obelisks alongside the railway track. The only activity those tracks ever saw were the few weeks of the year after harvest when freight trains carrying wheat would clunk along the tracks during the early hours of the morning.

After crossing the train line, we didn't actually realise it at first, but we were 'in town'. There was a main street, with a pub, a post office and a quaint-looking general store. I was extremely excited to see a twenty-five-metre swimming pool. I love swimming laps. But I soon learnt that it was only open in the summer season between four and seven p.m.

The next street over was Quandialla Central School. It was a lovely little place, with murals painted all over the walls and a sign proclaiming the school's mission: 'Together we provide opportunities to succeed.' Quandialla actually means 'echidna' in the local Aboriginal dialect, and I saw more than one echidna digging along the school's fence line in my time at the school.

The deputy principal met us out the front. He was a lovely man named Sam and he gave us a tour of the school. I was shocked to learn that there were no other English teachers at the school. The school population from kindergarten to Year 12 was about a hundred and twenty students in total, and many teachers taught multiple subjects. It turned out to be one sharp learning curve in the early days of my teaching career.

Sam then drove us three blocks over to show me the teacher's housing. In many rural towns, the Department of Education provides rental homes for teachers to encourage postgraduates like myself to come and teach in the country. It was a pretty bland sight, a clad box really, with an awful colour scheme of brown-on-brown-on-brown, but the rooms were big and there was a front porch with a wonderfully huge yard, just perfect for Hannah.

I agreed I would take on the job and move to Quandialla. We explained to Sam that we couldn't stay much longer, we had to get back to Sydney. He gave me the key to the house and we did the long trek home. Then my poor mother got up the next day and drove to Queensland. I don't think she got back in her car for a month after that.

I went home and set about organising for the next big chapter in my life. I hired a Budget truck and packed it up with my futon bed, a desk, some old furniture and bric-a-brac I'd accumulated: my beloved books, my CDs and my guitar. I rang Dad and informed him of my plans. My dad was so proud of me, the only member of my immediate family with a university degree and now starting a career in education. He had been a truck driver and knew most towns between Sydney and Perth but he hadn't been to Quandialla. He was keen to check it out, so I picked him up on my way through and with Hannah sitting up in the front cab between us, I moved to Quandialla.

Just as I had experienced when I moved to Newcastle and started uni all those years before, there was a vast chasm between expectation and realisation. The students at the school were absolutely beautiful. Behaviour management just wasn't a thing. They were beautifully mannered, hard-working, appreciative children of beautifully mannered, hard-working, appreciative farming stock. My teaching colleagues were so friendly and welcoming and supportive. But I found the first few months exceptionally tough. The culture shock, moving from Newtown to Quandialla, was rough. I didn't even have a car and if I wanted to buy groceries I needed to bum a ride into town which was a hundred-and-forty-kilometre round trip. Fortunately, the pub was within walking distance. I certainly spent a lot of time there.

I was so sad and lonely, drinking heavily and sobbing most nights, crying into the phone at my poor mother, telling her I'd done the wrong thing. I had taken the job on in term four, so by the end of the term it was Christmas break. I went north, taking Hannah on a plane with me, to spend the Christmas holidays with Mum. She revealed to me later that she didn't think she was going to get me back on the plane to go home to Quandialla, but fortunately, something clicked in me. I decided to return with a new attitude and throw myself into my new life.

The first thing I had to do was get a car. I was lucky that I had gotten my licence back in school but I'd never owned a car. I'd always been a city slicker. All I'd ever needed were two strong legs and my bicycle. But this was a totally new scenario, and I needed a car. A reliable car, not one of the dodgy old cars Dad offered to organise for me, like the Nissan Sunbird he told me I could buy off a mate of his that 'ran OK' but probably wouldn't start in the morning if the weather dropped below ten degrees.

Now that I had a permanent job and some earning power, I had a chat with the bank and took out a car loan. I had a grin from ear to ear that day I drove into town with my very own car: a white, two-door Toyota Echo. Of course, the staff and my kids thought it was hilarious, this six-footed Amazon woman and her big German shepherd driving around town, often with the guitar on the back seat, in this little 'mintie on wheels' as they called it, but I had that car for twenty years and it was still going strong when I finally sold it at a garage sale.

The second thing that made my stay in Quandialla much easier was meeting Susan. Susan was originally born in Quandialla and her family lived there, her parents on one farm, her brothers and their wives on surrounding farms. Susan had attended Quandialla Central School and had gone off to boarding school like a lot of farming students did for high school. Susan had then studied at the College of Fine Arts (COFA) in Sydney. But she'd recently moved back home to Quandialla to spend some time with her family after a bad break-up. (It seemed I wasn't the only one who still needed the loving arms of my mother even as a grown woman.)

Susan had tacked a Diploma of Education on the end of her arts degree, so she was doing some casual teaching at Quandialla Central School. At recess, the both of us had wandered out to the front of the school to hide from the students and smoke a cigarette and we hit it off instantly. That afternoon, we bonded over beers at the pub together and Susan quickly moved into the teacher's house with me. What followed were some of the wildest partying days of my life. Country kids know how to drink. And how to party. Our house down on Talbot Street was the local go-to when the pub closed, and most weeknights between Wednesday and Saturday we raised the roof until the sun came up. Music, beers and lots of laughter, there was always a row of utes sporting big aerials parked out the front of our place and RM-Williams-boot-cladded lads passed out all over the lounge room floor.

But Sunday afternoons were my favourite. Coming down after a week of partying, Susan would roll a joint and we'd have a few quiet beers, Susan drawing or painting at the kitchen table, me, with my guitar on my knees and Hannah at my feet, making up melodies and writing song lyrics in my scrapbooks. I adored Susan. We were kindred souls and she fired a creative spark in me that resulted in a period of prolific song writing.

A couple of years later, Susan started a serious relationship with a local boy, a sheep grazier whom she had known since school. They married and moved onto his family's farm. It was the right move for her. She was surrounded by her family and living on the land that she loved. She went on to have three children and start a lucrative business putting her extraordinary artistic skills to good use. But I found it hard to let go of Susan. I resented her desire to make her own journey that so clearly left me in the background.

Not that I didn't have some fuel in my own love bucket. During these wild party days, I'd hooked up with a man called Wayne. I've changed the names of absolutely everyone in this story to protect their privacy, but this man was actually named Wayne and I know that he won't mind me calling him by name.

Wayne lived at Bribbaree, some thirty kilometres away from Quandialla. I'd headed over there for a quiet drink one night, unaware that there was a bucks' night underway and the joint was jumping with a busload of intoxicated men. I've never had such a warm welcome on setting foot inside a pub in all my life. As soon as I opened the door, all eyes were on me, the only woman in the bar, and the boys started jeering and wolf whistling. It turned out they were waiting on a stripper they'd hired and they thought I was her! The stripper did eventually show up, but neither Wayne nor I watched her show. By then, we had got talking, and when the stripper started her performance, gyrating on the bar in a teeny pair of Union Jack boxer shorts, we moved outside to sit on the gutter, drinking schooners, smoking cigarettes and sharing a kiss.

The following week we met up again at the Quandialla Rodeo. Back then, the rodeo was one of the biggest days of the year for Quandialla, closely followed by the Quandialla Show. After a day at the showground, eating hot dogs, drinking beer and watching insane cowboy after insane cowboy risk their life for the chance to prove they could stay on top of a bucking bull for eight seconds, the crowd migrated over to the main street. The street was closed to traffic and a truck that converted into a stage was parked out the front of the Quandialla Hotel. Local bands played a set list of country covers and country girls and boys danced and drank until the sun came up. Wayne and I danced and danced, and when half the town ended up at our place on Talbot Street, he came along too.

Wayne was a big time 'cocky'. (Farmers are often called 'cockies'. Cockies are greedy birds that congregate on the roads feeding on grain that has fallen off the trucks carting it. They can even learn to unpick sacks to get at their favourite food, so grain farmers are also called cocky farmers because all they seem to do is grow grain to feed birds.) Wayne was, and still is, a 'good man'. Not long after I started seeing him, I had gone into town to do some shopping. Coming home in my little Echo, I ran over a nail-studded plank and got not one, but two, flat tyres. I'd been shown how to change a tyre but I didn't have two spares. I hitched a ride back into town and found Wayne. He drove me out to my car and repaired both those flats right there on the side of the road. I remember thinking, 'My knight in shining armour. Where've you been all my life?'

My dad referred to Wayne as a 'big player'. He wasn't the least bit interested in drugs, none of the country lads were, but boy could he drink! Wayne could even outdrink me. He was always the last man standing at the bar, and with Wayne I did some of my hardest drinking ever. And we really did have an awesome time. We were great mates (we still are) and we had loads of fun. We went camping and fishing. He even took me and my horse (yes, at Quandialla I was finally able to buy another horse!) up the Snowy Mountains for a week of camping, drinking and horse riding. And you can imagine the workout my Maton guitar got with all this partying.

My colitis hadn't packed up yet unfortunately. And having a colitis attack in Quandialla was the pits, let me tell you. The closest hospital was seventy kilometres away and they weren't equipped to handle me. One time, it got so bad I took a month off and went to Mum's, where I spent some time in hospital, coming home, once again, ashamed of my steroid-bloated face.

The years rolled on, as the years are wont to do. I look back on my time at Quandialla Central School as the best years of my teaching career. At a school like that, twenty years ago now, there was so much we were allowed to do that you just can't get away with any more. We took the kids camping, and abseiling, and caving, me taking my guitar and singing around the campfire with the kids after dinner. I even took Hannah. I have a photo the kids took one morning to prove it: me and Hannah curled up together, asleep in Wayne's swag. I was so involved with the school and having stayed there for six and a half years, I'd put a generation of students through high school, as the year advisor, girls' advisor, debating coach, end-of-year concert coordinator, excursion coordinator, SRC coordinator, the list is almost endless.

But in my life, there have been three horrendously traumatic events. I've already told you about the first one. I'm yet to tell you about the third one. But here's the second one.

Hannah was the perfect dog. In fact, she almost loved me too much. The biggest issue I had with Hannah was keeping her home. She was happy to sit at my feet all day but if I left her at home, to go to work for instance, she could scale a cyclone fence to come and find me. She knew where the school was. She even knew which classroom was mine. More than once, I'd be writing on the board and one of the kids would sing out, 'Miss Murphy, Hannah's at the door.' I'd turn around to find her smiling up at me as if to say, 'Aren't you happy to see me?'

Hannah also had a thunder phobia. In fact, any loud bangs would have her heart racing and her body trembling. If I was out in a thunderstorm, she would find me before the rain started hitting the bitumen. Because it wasn't sustainable to have me taking Hannah back home from school every other lesson, Wayne set up a run for her. We chained her to a long strip of hardy wire that gave her the entire run of the yard. She had fresh water and a swimming pool to sit in at one end and her kennel at the other.

One stinking hot day in early February, Quandialla Central School was having their swimming carnival at the local pool. I'd been there all morning, watching students dive off the blocks to the sound of the starter gun and timing laps on a stopwatch. When we took a break for lunch, I went home to check in on Hannah, like I often did.

As I came through the back gate, I was immediately surprised. She was usually there to greet me. My eyes followed the wire of her run until I saw, at the end of the run, her chain was over the other side of the fence. I knew, deep inside at that very moment, what I was going to find on the other side of that fence. The hairs on my arms are lifting and I can feel bile rising in my throat even to write about it now, all these years later. But I had to look. I had to walk over to the end of her chain and look over the fence.

Hannah had freaked out at the repetitive bang of the race starter gun. She'd tugged so hard at her chain she'd pulled a star post half out of the ground and she'd jumped the fence in an effort to run away. The saddest thing was, the chain didn't snap her neck and kill her instantly. Her back feet could actually touch the ground on the other side of that fence. Instead, she'd hung there in the heat of the day, unable to claw her way back over to the other side of the fence, and slowly died.

When I looked over the fence and I saw her blood-soaked tongue lolling out of her lifeless mouth, my legs collapsed beneath me. It was like a physical blow, I could barely breathe. I drove my car back to the main street, got out and collapsed on the road, trembling and gagging as though I was about to vomit. Some schoolkids found me and went racing off to find some teachers. Soon there was a crowd around me and someone even said, 'Is it Hannah?' without me having to say anything. They took me into the pub and poured two straight shots of whisky down my throat, rubbing my arms and putting a coat around me to stop me shivering despite the stifling heat.

Someone tracked Wayne down. He came and took me home. He cut Hannah down for me and quietly stood back as I held her stiff body and rocked her in my arms, sobbing again and again, 'I'm sorry. I'm sorry. I'm so, so sorry!'

Eventually, he told me gently, 'C'mon, Jude. You have to let her go.'

Wayne and I took Hannah out to his farm. We dug a hole for her on top of her favourite hill and covered her up.

The next four days, it took a gargantuan amount of effort to hold it together. I had a really important gig in town: a dinner and show concert with another musician and vocalist that I was being paid well for. My dad came out to stay with me and to attend the concert and a bunch of my workmates were coming too. I played my heart out that night, it was one of the most intense performances I've ever given. And the next day, I completely lost it, sobbing uncontrollably all day, and for days afterwards.

Wayne tried to console me. He reminded me that Hannah was up there on her favourite hilltop. He said she'd be happy there. He said she could spend the rest of her days chasing rabbits and kangaroos.

But for years after that, whenever a storm approached, I'd think about my poor, scared girl trembling in her grave to the sound of the rolling thunder.

10

Much as I loved teaching at Quandialla, the isolation of living there really wore me down. As you can imagine, it didn't take too long before a couple of heavy-drinking piss-wrecks like Wayne and I were on a collision course. We had some absolute 'donnybrooks', as my mum would say. One moment he was the love of my life and I was wearing an engagement ring. The next, I'd decided I couldn't spend the rest of my life married to a farmer and living on the land (and trust me, the drought didn't help matters any!) and I'd called the whole thing off. I really gave Wayne a terrible time.

I decided that I had to get out of Quandialla. I couldn't keep stringing Wayne along. I missed the action and the anonymity of the city, or at least a bigger town. I wanted to go to the movies and the theatre and see live music and read the paper over scrambled eggs in a trendy café on a Saturday morning. I wanted to do more travel. Wayne was happy to stay in the same town he'd been born in. And as for getting on a plane and seeing the world? Wayne was happy to keep his feet planted firmly on the ground. Not that he didn't love adventure. Wayne could pack a bag and some fishing rods and be out the door at a moment's notice. But we just wanted different things, and we had very different ideas about what constituted entertainment. Sometimes I wondered whether the only thing we had in common was alcoholism.

I had an application in for a transfer for what seemed like ages but nothing came through. So I decided that if I had to keep working there, I would at least move out of Quandialla. I bought my first home, a cute little cottage, in the cherry-picking town of Young, which was about seventy kilometres away from Quandialla. It wasn't as far away as I would have liked, but moving to Young from Quandialla was like moving to New York. I wasn't mad about the commute along kangaroo-infested roads but loads of people did it. Interestingly, in between buying the house and moving into it, my transfer came through, and I got offered the job at Young High School! Some things are simply meant to be. And Wayne and I didn't end there. It was pretty easy for Wayne to come into town and stay with me or for me to catch up with him out at Bribbaree. We kept dancing our on-and-off dance for a while yet.

Looking back now, Young was the next move my career needed, but it was truly a baptism of fire. After coming from a teaching post like Quandialla, where the students were so compliant and I was so well-established and, dare I say it, loved, Young High School was a tough gig. I was the new kid on the block, and consequently, every one of my classes were, shall we say, 'challenging' to say the least. I had no top classes, I didn't even have a senior class.

To make matters worse, one of the teachers in my faculty took an instant dislike to me. I discovered later she had vowed to 'bully me out of the staffroom' before she had even met me! It's astounding, I know, but there are people like that out there. She treated me horribly, misfeeding me information to make me look incompetent, criticising me in front of colleagues. It was a serious case of workplace bullying. I was an emotional wreck, breaking down in tears more than once during my first couple of months there, wishing I was still back at the gorgeous little school that was Quandialla Central. But I look back on this incident in my life with an enormous sense of pride now. I never stooped to her level. I held my head high, I dug in and got on with the job, and over time I earned the respect of my colleagues, some of whom remain close friends to this day.

Friday nights were big for us 'chalkies'. There was a pub in town that was even called the 'chalkie' pub because all the teachers drank there. That's where I was the Friday night Wayne came in to tell me my dad had died.

He could see that I was well into it. He asked me to come outside with him and I couldn't understand what he was on about.

'Have a drink,' I shouted at him. I carried on slugging at my beer and playing pool, but after a while I could see that something was wrong. Wayne wasn't ordering a beer. It didn't look like he was about to settle in.

He waited a little while and finally persuaded me to come outside.

'What's going on?' I asked him.

Wayne grabbed me by the shoulders and looked me in the eyes. 'Jude,' he said. 'Brendan passed away.'

'No…no, no, no, no, no!'

He held me firm as I thrashed about, trying to escape from his grip. People on the street dropped their heads and hurried past, suspecting, perhaps, that Wayne and I were having a fight. Wayne walked me to his ute and put me in the front seat, then went back inside to grab my bag and tell everyone that I was going home.

About ten years before Dad had died, he'd had a heart attack and had needed a quintuple bypass. Not only was heart disease in his DNA (all three of Dad's brothers had died of a heart attack) but the man drank like a fish, smoked like a trooper and ate bacon at virtually every meal. He didn't live the healthiest of lifestyles. But still, he was only sixty-four years old when he died, and it was a terrible shock.

In retrospect, the first few days after Dad died were quite beautiful. The grief, of course, was overwhelming, but my brother came down from Queensland and helped me arrange the funeral and clean out Dad's house. Mum came down for the funeral. She hadn't had any sort of amicable relationship with my dad for years, but she was there for us. When Anthony and I went to the 'viewing', going inside the little chapel to see Dad lying in the open casket (one of the hardest things I've ever had to do), Mum was there. I can remember looking at his face, smooth, like grey plastic, barely recognisable. I can remember bending down to kiss his forehead and gasping with shock when my lips met his ice-cold skin. That wasn't my dad in that cold room. My dad was gone.

That afternoon, Mum, Anthony, Wayne and I spent the afternoon at Aunty Vera's house. Aunty Vera, Uncle Ziggy and all the cousins came, and we talked and drank beers and watched the sun set over the Blue Mountains from Aunty Vera's front veranda. It was a really lovely afternoon.

The first few weeks after Dad died, I wandered around in a familiar bubble of bereavement. I didn't eat, couldn't sleep, I felt like I had nothing to say to anybody. I would walk along the hallways between classes watching the kids running, jostling, shouting and laughing, teachers hurrying off to class with books in their arms, and I'd wonder how the world could just carry on as normal. I wanted to scream, 'Don't you know my dad just died? How can you all just act like nothing has happened?' But of course, life goes on.

And life went on for me as well. I suppose it was fortunate that I had something to distract me: that is, planning a wedding. Dad had died in October and Wayne and I finally got married (seven years after we met) the following January. It was a warm evening down by Chinaman's Dam in Young, our friends and family gathered at the foot of the Japanese gardens. It was a really special wedding, very relaxed. Wayne and I even brought our dogs to the service; Wayne's little Jack Russell, Boss, dressed in a tuxedo that his mother made and my German shepherd, Mischa, with a big white bow around her neck.

After we married, Wayne and I lived in my little house in Young. I suppose this goes some way to explaining one of the big problems Wayne and I had. It was my house, I paid the mortgage and wouldn't let Wayne contribute to it in any way. Even as a married woman, I was fiercely independent, financially and emotionally. And Wayne had been born on the family farm and had grown up believing he would one day inherit it and carry on the family tradition. Sadly, the drought crushed that dream. On top of that, Wayne's father was diagnosed with an aggressive form of cancer, debilitating the once fighting fit farmer. Wayne's parents endured years of driving back and forth to specialists and hospitals, one unsuccessful operation after another. The family sold the farm, Wayne's parents moving in to a much smaller place in town. Poor Wayne was rudderless, having to leave behind two thousand acres to come and live in a pokey little cottage with his pig-headed wife in Young. He didn't even have enough room to park his motorbikes, much less his boat, his tractors, his windrowers, his tools… you get the idea. And neither one of us were easing back off the drinking, Wayne more than ever in a bid to escape his displacement and uncertainty.

A couple of years after we married, harvest time was approaching again. Wayne always disappeared for weeks at a time during harvest, taking his machinery north and hiring contractors to help him windrow crops day and night. Of course, this was the most important time of the year for farmers, generating their main source of income, but I always hated it. I'd be bored and lonely and I'd pine for Wayne, and sometimes I'd drive hundreds of kilometres in one weekend just to meet up with him for a couple of hours in the caravan, him usually too exhausted to do more than lie in my arms, snoring. So this particular year, I decided to do it differently. If Wayne was going away for weeks on end, so would I.

The first time I went overseas, I can remember my mum encouraging me to do a Contiki tour. 'No way!' I protested. I was way too cool at the ripe old age of twenty to do a Contiki tour. Aren't they just glorified school camps where the kids are allowed to drink and shag? But when I did my second trip, I was thirty-four years old. Contiki tours are for eighteen- to thirty-four-year-olds. I had six months before I wouldn't be eligible. So I took some long service leave and headed off, once again, for the other side of the world.

The first thing I did was head back to London, still just as in love with the place as I had been the first time I was there. I spent a week or two just immersing myself in the city, revisiting the sights, wandering through the markets, roaming through museums and art galleries, catching *Chicago* at West End. After a full day of sightseeing, I would find a cosy bar, have a couple of glasses of red wine and write in my journal, cutting and pasting all my little souvenirs from the day; tram tickets and train tickets and show tickets and museum pamphlets. My travel scrapbooks are some of my most valuable possessions.

Then it was in London that I hopped on a bus with a Contiki tour and spent a few weeks in Europe. And yes, it really was just like a school camp where the kids are allowed to drink and shag! There were some complete dicks on the tour, but I was old enough to stay clear of all of that, and I didn't regret doing the Contiki tour for one minute. There's no way I could have travelled so much ground and have seen so many sights for that sort of price if I had done it on my own. Between visiting Anne Frank's house in Amsterdam, seeing the Glockenspiel in Munich, eating sauerkraut and drinking pints of ale in the Hauffrahaus in Germany, riding a gondola in Venice, looking out over the Vatican City from the top of St Peter's Bascillica, seeing *David* in Florence, and that was just the tip of the iceberg. And there were also plenty of lovely people on that tour. My room-mate was a girl named Melinda, a down-to-earth daughter of a dairy farmer on the South Coast. She was a lot younger than me but we got on like a burning house.

When we arrived in Paris, the tour was destined to return to London, but I left the tour and stayed in Paris for what was to be the highlight of my trip, catching up with my dearest friend, Pete.

I had known Pete since school, and we spent a lot of time together after school as we both lived in the city. When I was still at uni, Pete decided to go on a trip to Africa and she just never came home. But Pete and I had always kept in touch, writing long letters to each other that were almost novellas, documenting our highs and lows, sharing our darkest secrets. After Africa, Pete lived for a time in a cave in Tenerife, then moved on to a hippy commune in Spain. Pete was, and is, unlike anyone I've ever known.

I hadn't seen Pete for ten years when we met up in Paris, but when we fell into each other's arms and started babbling at each other, it was like we'd never been apart. For the next couple of days, Pete and I did Paris. We rummaged through second-hand shops, trying on shoes and scarves and glamorous dresses, we drank champagne and ate macaroons, we watched the sun set over Paris from the top of the Arc De Triomphe, and we just talked and talked and talked.

Pete left Paris to return to her home in the hills, a few hours outside of Barcelona. She had vegies in the garden to water and jewellery to make and artwork to create that she could sell at the markets. I went to Spain as well, but I didn't stay with Pete. Instead, I spent a week in Barcelona, in a hotel just back from La Calle Rambla.

I had studied conversational Spanish at university and had always been obsessed with the language. It was so exciting to actually be using Spanish, to sit in a café and order eggs and toast and *café con leche* and have everything arrive just as I'd ordered without a word of English! I can remember on one of my last days in Barcelona, lying on the bed in the hotel room watching a movie in Spanish and realising that I was actually able to follow what was going on. I was miserable to leave Spain. It felt wrong. I felt like I should be finding a job, renting out a funky little apartment and living out the rest of my days eating paella and strolling along *la playa*.

But I said adios to Spain and continued on my way. My trip wasn't quite over. I had a week stopover in New York before touching ground again in Sydney. The first thing I did in New York was buy a brand-new pair of sneakers as I'd completely walked through the soles of my old ones. And New York was such a wonderful way to spend the end of my trip, walking every block of Manhattan and drinking in the oh-so-familiar sights of that famous city, taking a ferry out to see the Statue of Liberty, roaming through the Guggenheim Museum, standing at the top of the Empire State Building, eating pretzels and pizzas. I couldn't stop laughing at the broad Bronxy accents of the taxi drivers and I couldn't believe how cold it was in New York, even as early as November.

But I'll never forget my last night in New York City. I was having a beer in the bar at the hotel where I was staying, just up from Times Square. I struck up a conversation with a lovely man named Jack. We talked for hours and somehow the conversation entered murky waters for me. Jack asked me some pretty confronting questions about who I really was and what I really wanted. When he asked me why I would have spent a couple of months on the other side of the world without my husband, I completely broke down. I knew that Wayne had missed me horrendously. The couple of times I'd spoken to him on the phone over the past couple of months he'd sounded like he wasn't coping at all. I'd been telling everyone that the reason I'd done the trip without him was that he'd been too busy with harvest. But the truth was, I'd wanted the time away from him. I'd wanted to do it on my own.

I remember later that night ringing my mum from a phone booth in Times Square. I was completely distraught, wondering how on earth I was going to get on the plane the next day and come home. Mum assured me it was perfectly normal to feel this way after a major trip, that it would take some readjusting but that everything would be okay. But I knew, in the hollows of my heart, I knew that it went much deeper than that. I returned to my hotel room and cried inconsolably, unable to catch a wink of sleep. I knew that Wayne and I were over and I was going to have to go home and end my marriage.

11

Wayne didn't make it easy for me. If only he'd been angry, or hateful, or hurtful, it might have been easier. But Wayne doesn't have a mean bone in his body. For months after the split, I would wake every Saturday morning to the sound of Wayne leaving the paper and a coffee at the back doorstep for me before getting back in his ute and driving off to work. Sometimes he'd leave a bunch of fresh tomatoes and zucchinis in a plastic bag; gifts from his mother's vegie patch.

I knew it would be impossible to stay in Young. Wayne's family was huge and they all lived there. Our wide circle of friends all lived there. I'd been toing and froing in my relationship with Wayne for the ten years over which I'd known him. It was impossible not to like him, not to love him. Any time I felt down or got lonely, I knew he'd be there, and I was too selfish not to take advantage of that. I had to be a grown-up, and let it go.

Fortunately, a few things fell into place that helped me transition into the next phase of my life. A colleague I worked with had always loved my house. When he heard I was selling, he offered to buy it. We arranged everything privately and I didn't even have to go through a real estate agent. I applied for a job in Bathurst, went for the interview and landed a position at Bathurst High School. I found myself a cute little house and Mischa and I moved to Bathurst.

I settled in to the town of Bathurst really quickly. It was so exciting to live somewhere that had a movie cinema, an indoor aquatic centre, a music conservatorium and an entertainment centre. I would take myself off to the theatre to watch plays and live shows. I'll never forget swooning to the Russian Ballet Company performing *Swan Lake*. And I loved my new house. I quickly set about making it mine, knocking a wall out here, building a shelf there, putting down new carpet and painting the walls with rich, warm colours: Burgundy red in the lounge-room, Amazon green in the bedroom. I loved my garden, spending the weekends mowing the lawn, weeding the garden beds and then sitting in the sun on my front porch with Mischa, reading a book and sinking pots of tea.

The first year after leaving Young was a time of enormous growth. I felt really strong and confident, proud of the way I'd earned a new job on merit, proud that I was making mature decisions I believed were setting me on the path of spiritual development. People said I seemed to glow, exuberant with a sense of inner harmony. I truly believed I would be rewarded for the courage of my convictions. I felt open-minded, receptive to the infinite possibilities the rest of my life had to bring. That's probably why I was such a perfect candidate for the evil clutches of the man who was about to enter, and almost end, my life.

I wouldn't write his name here, even if I could. But I can't write his name. I can't even say his name. For the purposes of this narrative, let's just call him Fuckhead.

It might sound strange, but I need to start this part of the story by telling you about my hair. Some time before I turned thirty and was back living in Quandialla, I noticed something was going on with my hair. I've never been pretty, but one thing I always had was beautiful hair: long, curly locks I'd dye henna red, so thick I could barely twist a hairband around a ponytail twice. Everybody commented on my hair. 'It's your best asset,' a friend told me. 'With hair like that, you could have any man you wanted,' said another. (Untrue, for the record.) Wayne adored my hair, often bunching it up in his fists and kissing me passionately, groaning, 'Fuck, I love your hair.'

And then one day, in the shower, washing my mane, I noticed my hands were full of long strands. 'Hhhhhmmmm, strange,' I thought. I combed conditioner through it, as I always did, and more clumps of hair were coming out in the comb. I was alarmed but tried to stay calm. 'Perhaps it needs a trim,' I thought.

Over the next few days, more than the average amount of hair was coming out in my hands every time I touched my hair. When I whipped it up into a ponytail, I was certain it felt thinner and more straggly than usual. I booked myself in for a haircut.

When I sat in the hairdresser's chair, I told her my concerns.

'Well,' she assured me breezily, 'it's quite normal to lose up to three hundred strands of hair a day.' She proceeded to pin my hair up and started to snip away. And then she said, 'So, you've got a bit of alopecia happening here.'

Alo-what? I had no idea what she was talking about and I told her so.

'Alopecia.' She got a hand mirror and held it up behind my head, showing me a patch about as big as a fifty-cent piece at the back of my skull.

I gasped in shock and my bottom lip began to tremble. The young hairdresser went off for a moment and came back with the manager. Together they both stood behind me, inspecting my bald patch as tears started rolling down my cheeks.

'What is it?' I managed to ask between sobs.

'Well,' started the manager, 'it's alopecia. Hair loss. At the moment, it looks pretty concentrated in one area, but you could wake up tomorrow with no hair, no eyebrows...'

'What causes it?' I wanted to know.

'Well, sometimes new medication. Or stress. Have you been under a lot of stress lately?'

'Well, I fucking am now!' I blurted out.

The hairdresser finished trimming my hair, I paid the bill and wandered off to find a phone and ring my mum.

'Mum, my hair is falling out!' I cried.

My mum's initial reaction was to laugh. 'Jude, you've got more hair than a lion. I'm sure you can afford to lose a bit of hair.' She just couldn't seriously consider me losing my hair. She couldn't connect with my terror, my nightmarish visions of waking up the next day completely bald, looking like something out of Roald Dahl's *The Witches*.

It took me twenty-four hours before I shaved my head. I would be controlling my hair, thank you very much. It wouldn't be controlling me, even though shaving it exposed the big bald patch at the back of my head that got considerably worse before getting any better. And everyone told me that I wore the pixie cut well, I was an inspiration, Wayne and the gang at Quandialla pub raising their beers to me: 'Cheers, big ears!' But behind my back I knew they were tutting in sympathy. 'Such a shame,' they said. Some of the school students were in tears, believing I had cancer. My mum introduced me to some of her workmates saying, 'This is my daughter, Jude. She used to have beautiful hair, just like Nicole Kidman's.' And she'd pull a photo out of her wallet.

I'd kept it short for a couple of years, patches popping up here and there. I'd tried to grow it long again and succeeded to get it down to my shoulders until the alopecia returned, clumps of hair in my hands, a hairball in the shower drain the size of a small cat. Ever since then, I've had super-short hair.

And do you know the first words he said to me? The night I met Fuckhead, a man who'd never known me with long, glorious hair? Of all the things he could have said, of all the pick-up lines he could have spun, can you guess the first words he said to me? 'I like your hair.'

I was out on the town with a bunch of schoolteachers I'd met through my new job. We were having a farewell for a young colleague who had scored a teaching position in Japan. The more sensible among us had already called it a night, but a few of us were kicking on, crawling pubs. I'd had a skinful, but my thoughts were clear and my mouth was mine, speech still sharp and in control.

And in he marched. Regal. He seemed a giant, owned the space. He wore an army-green coat and floated with the confidence of a man who knew all eyes were on him, drinking in his difference, his exoticness. His hard-set, chiselled jaw, his profile, like some warrior, his lips, pursed in defiance, unwilling to part with words just for the sake of it.

The band was awful, rockabilly shit, and the music was way too loud. Everyone was yelling at each other, only catching snippets of each other's conversations, bodies bumping up against each other on the dance floor. My mates told me they were moving on to another pub. It was too late in the evening and I was too drunk to invent an excuse. I said goodbye, stumbled over and sat on the chair next to him.

He helped me onto it, holding the stool steady while I balanced my wine glass on the bar and mounted. His face hardly changed. He just jutted his chin forward in a quick whip of acknowledgment, as if to say, 'I see you've finally made it, I've been waiting for you.' We probably said hello and told each other our names, but the first thing I can remember him saying is, 'I like your hair.'

I took him home. He spilt beer all over my lounge room floor and told me I was amazing. We got half naked, writhing on the lounge room floor when something inside my addled brain clicked, remembering suddenly (and fleetingly, as it turned out), that I was in a better place, I was stronger, that I didn't want to be giving myself away so easily. I pulled away and told him to leave. He asked for my number so I gave it to him, then kicked him out and went to bed. Woke proud. Powerful. Evolved, I thought. Hun.

He called me a couple of days later, teasing me with that accent, those chopped, unusual, poetically placed words. 'I want you to be my queen,' he told me.

Part of me thought him ridiculous, but he flattered me. And it was just so different. So different to Wayne, so different to anyone I'd ever been with.

I let him take me out, buy me a drink, tell me his story. And he spun his yarn with all the charm of Othello; a poor village, a cruel father, poverty, violence, the Western women who had done him wrong, the one who married him and had his two children but turned out to be a 'rich white bitch' but would always win because that was the plight of the black man, a battle all the way, and like the smitten Desdemona, 'with greedy ear I did devour up his discourse…paid his pains a world of sighs' and I seethed with hatred and indignation at the injustice and intolerance and narrow-mindedness of her, of all of them. But I was better. Softer. If only he would wrap his battle-weary arms around me, I could nurse his wounds and give him comfort. I could be his queen.

Fuck... I was such an idiot.

12

To borrow a cliché, I was putty in Fuckhead's hands. I'd check my phone obsessively, wilting if I hadn't heard from him, spirits soaring when his name popped up in my message box. Because money meant everything to Fuckhead, he worked two jobs; by day, labouring at a metal workshop, by night, packing shelves at a supermarket. We didn't really see each other during the week, but on a Friday and Saturday night Fuckhead would come over after his shelf-packing job. I'd wait up, constantly checking my phone for the message to tell me he'd finished work and was heading over. It was rarely before midnight, sometimes not until the early hours of the morning. He always told me he'd been held back, but I discovered, too late unfortunately, that Fuckhead had plenty of interests other than me.

And if I'm honest with myself, the warning signs were there. He could be affectionate in private but when we were out in town, he was cold and closed, and always seemed to be scanning the crowd, and I half wondered whether he was afraid to be seen with me. He loved to go for long drives, but I always had to be behind the wheel. No matter the time of day, he'd bring a six-pack of beer and sit in the passenger seat drinking one after the other. In hindsight, I believe this fulfilled his fantasy of being chauffeured around, like the well-to-do men he might have watched from afar as a poor child in his village.

He was jealous too. I admit, I found this a little flattering at first, that he thought I was such an object of desire for other men. But it got ridiculous. One Christmas Eve, I went out with friends and we arranged to meet at the pub when he finished work. When he arrived and I was chatting to a male work colleague, he was seething, accusing me of flirting. He wouldn't talk to me or touch me for the rest of the night. His comments about my appearance were incomprehensible. One day he'd say I looked 'sexy' and 'fresh'. The next day he'd instruct me to change my clothes because he thought they were too revealing, and he'd criticise me for wearing make-up or colouring my hair. 'Why do you have to look so fancy?' he demanded. 'Who are you trying to impress?' And I remember that same Christmas, I spent hundreds of dollars on him, buying him clothes and expensive trainers he wanted. As a present, he gave me four bunches of half dead flowers that the supermarket was obviously giving away to staff the day before Christmas.

But just when it seemed he was tossing me out, he'd reel me back in. Just when I thought the way he was treating me was unacceptable, he'd turn on the charm, telling me in that Rastafarian lingo that he loved me 'body, mind and soul'. 'I wish I'd met you years ago,' he'd tell me. 'I would have had a good life.' He'd explain away his jealousy and paranoia by reminding me of his abusive childhood and his philandering father. He had a lump in his throat, a bullet lodged there since he was boy, and other bullets throughout his body. What untold horrors had he seen? How could I ever blame him for being guarded and for never having a role model to teach him how to love, and be loved?

Fuck... I was an idiot.

And then Fuckhead started talking about a baby. I was thirty-seven years old by then. I'd never, ever wanted a baby. I'd been married to Wayne, who would have loved a baby, but the idea had never appealed to me. It probably doesn't take Einstein to figure out that I had issues with the idea of being responsible for another life, given my history. But I was selfish, too. I loved my free and easy life, coming and going as I pleased. I loved my dogs. I loved the kids I taught at school. I didn't need a child of my own. But Fuckhead wouldn't let up. 'Let's make a baby,' he'd say, again and again. 'I know we're going to be together forever. I know we're going to be a family.' He wouldn't let up, saying it over and over again, placing his hand on my stomach and staring into my eyes. 'Let's make a baby,' he'd whisper, kissing me deeply. And before I'd really thought about it, we were having sex without protection.

And I prayed for a baby. I wanted to be pregnant more than anything in the world. The split second my period was overdue, I took a pregnancy test, staring at the little stick and willing two pink lines to emerge in the window. I so wanted a baby. Not just a baby. His baby. I fantasised over and over about telling him that we were having a baby. I wanted to see the adoring look on his face when I told him we were to become a family. Up to this point, Fuckhead still had his own place, a house he had bought with his ex-wife I knew where it was but I was never invited there. He only ever came to my place. I thought, if I'm having his baby, surely he'll move in here with me. Surely we could start living together.

And it happened. Quickly. I think I knew before the pregnancy test confirmed it. My nipples were tingling. I felt different. And when those two pink lines emerged in the window, I was awash with ecstasy.

I didn't want to tell Fuckhead over the phone. I wanted to tell him in person. I drove over to his house and knocked on the door, my heart thumping in my chest with nervousness and excitement. I pictured him picking me up off the ground and swinging me in his arms. I'd make him so happy with the news, that he would get what he wanted, that we had 'made a baby'.

At first, he seemed shocked to see me at the door. Then annoyed. For a moment, I wasn't even sure he was going to let me come in, but after a while I followed him inside, past the piles of clothes and junk on the hallway floor and into the kitchen. It looked for all the world as though a party had just taken place. There were empty beer bottles and wine bottles, unwashed wine glasses making red-stained rings on the kitchen bench. (He didn't drink red wine.) There were dishes everywhere. There was an ashtray with cigarette butts in it. (He didn't smoke cigarettes.) There were takeaway food boxes all over the floor. I took it all in, a million questions bubbling up within me. But I said nothing.

I moved to hold him, kiss him. I wanted to be sure the mood was right when I told him our incredible news. But he looked tired and seemed preoccupied. Knowing what I know now, there's every chance there was another woman in his bedroom.

'So…' I began. 'I'm pregnant. We're going to have a baby.'

Fuckhead looked at me, and the strangest expression settled over his face. He sort of smirked, as though I'd just told him a joke. He didn't seem at all excited. He didn't move to hold me or kiss me. Instead, he raised his eyebrows, tilted his head and said, 'Well…congratulations.'

Congratulations? A strange sensation came over me, like ice running underneath my skin. It wasn't what I'd expected at all. I had visions of him dropping to his knees, kissing my stomach and telling me he loved me. Where was the man who had been hounding me and hounding me for a baby? Where was the man who told me he was going to look after me forever, that we were going to get married and be a family? Where was the man who asked me to be his *queen*?

But like I would do a thousand times over the next nine months, I made excuses for him. Perhaps he's just tired. I guess it's my fault, expecting him to be happy to see me when I didn't warn him I was coming, when I showed up unexpectedly like this. Maybe he's just overwhelmed by the news. Perhaps it's a cultural thing. Maybe African men have a different way of displaying their emotions. Maybe, without meaning to, I've rehashed some confronting feelings in him about his other children. I know he loves me. Everything will be fine.

Fuck… I was such an idiot.

Some time later, Fuckhead moved into my place. He continued to run hot and cold, his affection and attention towards me as inconstant as the moon. One day he couldn't get enough of me, showering me with compliments and talking, with such certainty and confidence, about our bright future as a family. Then he'd spend day after day in my garage, completely ignoring me, listening to music, drinking beer and cooking revolting, repulsive-smelling concoctions. He called them his 'African recipes', huge pots with goat's feet sticking out the top, hooves still attached. He'd come and go at all different hours and I was never able to predict what mood he'd be in. Jubilant and affectionate? Or sullen and irritated?

And he never stopped talking about money. Namely, his lack of it. Despite working two jobs, he never seemed to have any money. He was renting his house out and getting money for that, he was paying no rent and not contributing to the bills at my house, but he never had any money. He complained about his 'gold-digging' ex-wife and the expense of his kids. He said he had to send money back home, to his mother and brothers in Africa. He'd tell me he needed to borrow money to put new tyres on his car so that he could get it registered, could I loan him the money and he'd pay me back? I'd give it to him and then he'd come home with a case of beer. He told me he needed tens of thousands of dollars to pay his ex-wife and buy their house outright, that it would be an investment for our child. And I gave it to him.

Because, fuck… I was such an idiot.

And there were those phone calls. So many long, long phone calls. He'd lie on the floor in front of his laptop, skyping people back home, speaking in his own language, knowing I didn't understand. His brothers, he said, but the conversations didn't sound casual or friendly. They were fierce. Aggressive. He was angry, argumentative, yelling and sometimes smashing his fists on the floorboards next to his computer screen.

On the rare occasion that he did show interest in my growing belly, he referred to our baby as his boy. His son. We were going to name him 'Ziggy.'

'What if it's a girl?' I asked.

He looked at me like I had two heads. 'No, it's a boy,' he'd say.

And I had a scan at twenty weeks. And I found out the sex of the baby. A girl. And that's when he really lost interest. And I knew. Deep in the guts of me I knew I was doomed. I knew I was on my own. And I so wish I'd told him to leave then. But I just couldn't. I couldn't admit that I'd made such a terrible mistake. I couldn't admit that I'd been so, so stupid. I was an independent, intelligent, professional woman, wasn't I? How could I have let this happen? I couldn't do this on my own. And maybe, maybe when the baby arrives, and he meets her, he'll fall in love with her and he'll remember how much he loves me and then, then we'll be a family. Everything will be fine.

Yep… I was such an idiot.

13

I can't blame Fuckhead for all my pregnancy woes. The mental and emotional trauma he caused me was criminal. In fact, I keep expecting to turn on the television one night and see a story about him on *A Current Affair*, his dreadlocked head plastered all over the screen, the dramatic voice over warning women about this 'philandering, cheating, lying, con man with serial impregnator syndrome'. (Yes, serial impregnator syndrome is actually a thing. I saw it on *Law and Order*.)

But I had other problems to worry about. Even in the early days of my pregnancy, I thought that all the women who had ever been pregnant before must have been tough as nails. It seemed to me to be constant pain. Not just morning sickness (although I had that in spades) but horrendous cramps, like worse than the worst period pain. I bled quite a bit, on and off, once so bad I was convinced I'd lost the baby. I went up to the hospital and they sent me for an ultrasound, but there she was, a little jellybean on the screen, heart beating away. But as I grew bigger, my god, the agony. I felt like a too-full balloon was being blown up beneath my skin. The pain beneath my ribs and in my back was so bad I'd lie on the floor moaning, feeling like the excruciation would have me vomiting any minute.

In the last trimester, I hardly slept. I would lie down in bed and close my eyes but something seemed to have broken in my brain. My sleep switch was stuck. It wouldn't turn on, and I'd just get up again and go out in the lounge room, turn the television on low and pace around the kitchen or lie down on the floor, praying I might just float off, but I rarely did.

I was also admitted to hospital around this time for yet another colitis attack. Many women with colitis or Crohn's actually experience a reduction in symptoms during pregnancy, but I wound up on a drip and a cocktail of more anti-inflammatories.

Some time in the last trimester, they found the cyst. I was enormous, and crippled with constant pain, and I had a big bleed. I got out of the shower one morning, I was about to get ready for school, and I felt a warmth between my legs. I looked down to find rivers of blood streaming down the inside of my thighs and pooling on the floor. I rushed up to the hospital, the nurses tying a heart monitor around my tummy. I was sure the baby was dead, but there she was, her heart still beating, unstoppable. But they sent me for an ultrasound.

There I was, yet again. I'd lost count by now of the number of times I'd been lying there on that table, the nurse gliding her wand over the cold, sticky gel on the bulge of my baby. But this one was different. This time she held the wand in one spot too long, click-clicking on her computer, turning the wand this way and that way, asking me to move around. Eventually, she excused herself for a moment and left the room, returning with two doctors. They all stood there, grunting and umming and aahing over the grainy, black photographs on the monitor. At last, they'd found the source of all that pain. A big, black shadow in my 'upper left quadrant', a blob, a cyst.

It was enormous, as big as the baby, and with the baby almost full term, they couldn't really tell what was going on. They thought it was probably attached to the bowel but they didn't really know. And suddenly I was a 'high risk' case. A team of four doctors was created and I had to go up to the hospital every couple of days to meet with them and be reviewed. One of the doctors recommended I have a Caesarean, but the other three suggested that natural labour would be better. It would pose less risk to the baby. And how I wish I'd listened to that doctor and insisted on a Caesarean. But of course, once doctors start telling you what's best for the baby, well…

The last few weeks before the birth, I was insane with pain and insomnia. When I moved, white lights flashed before my eyes. I had bleeds so often I even stopped going up to the hospital, afraid they'd seen so much of me they thought me a nuisance. In fact, when I actually went into labour, I didn't even know it.

My neighbour, Mel, had come over for a cup of tea. As I was speaking to her, I kept stopping to close my eyes and catch my breath. Mel said to me, 'Jude, you're in labour. You need to go to the hospital.'

Fuckhead was at home. He was doing weights or something in the garage. He dropped me off at the hospital and told me he was going home for a shower and he'd be back soon. He was literally hours. I suppose he stopped in for a rendezvous with one of his other women. It's very likely, given that I discovered, a year after my daughter was born, that he already had another woman pregnant.

Fortunately, I had Mel. She stayed with me at the hospital until Fuckhead finally showed up, sitting quietly as I stood next to the bed, swaying and stamping my feet, breathing and hissing in the grip of each contraction.

And it was going well. I was doing well, working with the pain. The contractions were close together now, and the nurse took me to the labour ward and did an examination. I was fully dilated, ready to go, managing the pain with an occasional suck on the gas. But things weren't moving. They did another examination. The head was engaged but my waters hadn't broken. The nurse got an instrument that looked like a knitting needle, digging inside me until I screamed for her to stop but then I felt the sudden warmth gushing over my thighs. They stood me up again and told me to push. They dimmed the lights and rolled a tiny crib into the room, padded with a pink and blue striped hospital blanket. I can remember looking up at the clock. It was about six o'clock at night and I heard one of the nurse's say, 'Well, we know this baby's birthday.' And it was such a strange feeling, looking at that crib and imagining seeing my baby there, any minute. If only my baby came then.

But then something changed. The pain changed. I knew that things were going wrong. It was the pain of the cyst. Something had moved. The baby and the cyst, it wasn't right. That full balloon beneath my skin so taut I thought my guts would explode. And I screamed and the nurses seemed to be angry with me. 'Don't you feel like bearing down?' they kept asking me, but I had no idea what they were talking about. All I felt was cracking pain, high up in my guts, like a fire, like the slice of a knife. The baby's head had floated away and it was the cyst that was engaged, and there was no way I would be giving birth to that cyst, today or any other day. And they sounded as though they thought it was my fault. And I'd never been pregnant before, I'd never had a baby before. How was I to know that none of this was normal?

And then the nightmare really began. They put me in a bath and Fuckhead had to sit beside me and hold my head above the water and stop me smashing my head against the side of the bath as I thrashed about like a marlin on a hook. Then they put me on a birthing chair, and I pushed and pushed and shat myself in front of Fuckhead and the nurses and then…the clock passed midnight.

And that's when I truly lost it. They had told me that my baby would be born the day before, but now it was the next day, so none of them knew what they were doing, they were feeding me lies and I couldn't trust anybody. I looked around at the faces of the people who were watching me go through more pain than I thought humanly possible and I stood up and I walked right through a pile of my own shit and I got up on the bed and became totally, completely, textbook case hysterical.

I started screaming, 'I'm not doing this any more! I want some fucking pain relief now! You get the doctor up here now. I want some fucking pethidine!' I roared like a bear in a trap and suddenly all the lights came on and that dimly lit crib disappeared and it seemed every nurse in the hospital was in that room and I was lying on my side and the contractions were zero seconds apart, smashing me and smashing me, and I was gripping the bed head and bellowing and the nurse was trying to make eye contact with me and talk me down but I'd lost it and I wouldn't listen to anyone.

One of the nurses said the doctor was on his way and I felt so betrayed by this room full of tormentors that I didn't even believe her. I grabbed the woman's arm and screamed at her, 'Promise me! You promise me the doctor is on his way!' That's where I was, in my head. I was in a room full of people who knew I was going to die and they were lying to me. That's what I truly thought.

And it took that doctor a good forty-five minutes to arrive while I was in a constant state of contraction, volcanic explosions of pain pulverising me. And by the time he arrived, he tried to give me the preamble about the risks related with having an epidural and I screamed at him, 'Shut up and stick it in!' And oh, sweet Jesus, the relief was almost immediate and I prayed to God, 'Thank you,' and I felt like maybe, just maybe, I would live. And then a different doctor was down there with a vacuum and he was pushing the cyst out of the way and trying to find the baby's head and draw her out and the nurses were placing their hands on my belly so they could feel the contractions and telling me to push and breathe and push and breath and I did. I did exactly what they told me to do again and again, and then I heard Fuckhead say, 'Here it comes, here comes your baby,' and even then, even in the midst of that horrific traffic accident that was the delivery of my baby, I felt socked, punched in the face by his words. She was *my* baby, but not his.

But then, they placed Sienna on my chest. And I remembered why I was there. I was having a baby. And they took my gown off me and placed my daughter on my chest and the world stood still. When I looked at Sienna, I just forgot everything, even him. In that moment, it was just me and that baby. And I'd been torn into next Tuesday and the doctor was down there stitching me up and nurses were fluffing around with tubes and needles but I just looked into her eyes and I fell in love. Like never before. That tiny head, small as a mandarin. That caramel skin, those huge brown eyes and long eye lashes, like a gentle dairy cow. And she wasn't even crying. She just looked up at me, calmly, and blinked. And then she latched on. And the next few hours were probably the happiest of my entire life. If I was granted the opportunity to relive just one hour from my whole life, it would be the first hour I held my daughter.

14

After Sienna was born, I still looked pregnant. The cyst moved now, had shifted into the space where Sienna had been, an enormous blob like a water-filled balloon. I could actually pick it up and move it around with my hands. My team of surgeons made some follow up appointments for me to come back and organise its removal, and after four days, they let me take my baby home. I'd been crying non-stop and hadn't slept a wink.

I don't know where Fuckhead was. Working? Drinking? Shagging? It doesn't matter, but the worst thing was, because everyone assumed I had a partner, no one suspected that I might be struggling on my own. My mother hadn't spoken to me since I told her I was pregnant. She would deny it, I'm sure, but she was horrified by my relationship with a black man, and she had old-fashioned, Catholic-influenced ideas about having a baby out of wedlock.

I remember very little about the first few days after bringing Sienna home. I know my insomnia was out of this world. When you're expecting a baby everybody says, 'Get used to feeling tired, you won't get any sleep.' But it wasn't like that. Sienna was sleeping. She slept round the clock. I even had to wake her for feeds. But I could not fall asleep. Day and night, my sleep switch was broken.

I do remember one afternoon, with Sienna snoring away in her crib, I opened Fuckhead's laptop to search for a baby sling I could buy online. His internet history popped up, showing filthy porn site after filthy porn site, close-up shots of huge, wet vaginas assaulting me from his laptop screen. And even worse, internet dating sites. He was on half a dozen of them and had been chatting to potential partners as recently as that morning. It seems so stupid to say I was shocked, but I was. It also seems so stupid to admit that I didn't even tell him to leave then and there. I should have, but I simply didn't have the energy at that point to do it. There were still too many things for me to work through.

Seven days after the birth, I went to see my GP. I looked like death. I hadn't been eating, I could barely stomach water, and I was so sleep-deprived I'd actually started hallucinating. I kept hearing things, a whoosh in my ears like a crashing wave. And I was seeing things in my peripheral vision. Spots and stars and streaks of black, like a cat darting across the floor, but I'd turn to look and there was nothing there. My eyes stung. My head felt ready to split from cracking migraines. I'm sure my breast milk hadn't come in and I'm sure Sienna was anything but a settled baby with her mother in the grip of post-natal psychosis. Looking back, it's here that I should have been admitted to a psychiatric hospital, but I had too much going on. I had to get this cyst out.

My GP prescribed Zyprexa, an antipsychotic. The worst thing was, I couldn't breastfeed on this medication. The doctor informed me that I would have to express my milk and tip it out, feeding Sienna formula for the next few days. Of course, she wasn't to know that it would take more than a few days on Zyprexa to straighten me out, but if only someone had said to me,' Jude, in this case, it's OK for you not to breastfeed. It's OK for you to feed your baby formula while you concentrate on getting well.' If only someone had given me permission to do that. But there was such a push from all directions to breastfeed. 'Breast is best!' screamed posters in the maternity ward. I went home with my medication and without the first clue about how to feed my baby formula.

The wife of a colleague I worked with was a neonatal nurse. I'd met her a number of times through my colleague. I rang her now and explained what was happening and asked for her help. She came to my aid, thank goodness. She helped me buy a breast pump and formula and bottles and teats and a steriliser and told me how to use it all. I don't think my milk had properly come in anyway. It seemed to take forever to pump the tiniest amount and it was heart-breaking to then tip it down the sink.

I took the Zyprexa. It didn't really help me fall asleep. It was more like being slammed between the eyes with a sledgehammer. I'd lie down, my head swirling and body trembling and vibrating with a feeling like terror, then I'd wake to find I'd been asleep for an hour or two. But there were times over the next few weeks when even Zyprexa wouldn't knock me out.

The operation to remove my cyst had been scheduled for about four weeks after the birth. They were planning on cutting my belly wide open to get it out. In the meantime, it was growing. I looked as though I was nine months pregnant, and the pain was constant. I felt sick, not surprisingly because, as I later learned, the cyst had ruptured and toxins were pumping around my body. I also learned later, when I finally found out it was actually attached to my ovary and not the bowel as they originally thought, that my hormones were completely out of whack. That certainly wasn't helping my acute mental state.

And this is the point in my story where I always stop and say a silent prayer of thanks. Thank you, God, for Dr Andrew Mackendar, the gastroenterologist who had seen me through a bunch of colitis attacks, who had been the doctor on my team of surgeons who had championed for that Caesarean, and the doctor who rang me now and begged me not to go ahead with the operation they had planned for me at Bathurst Base Hospital. I remember him saying to me, 'Put it this way, Jude, if you were my wife, I wouldn't let you go through with this surgery.' He urged me to travel to Orange and meet with a colleague of his, another gastro-surgeon, who was making a name for himself doing amazing things via laparoscopy. I did as he asked, and I'm so glad I did.

Because the cyst wasn't what they'd been expecting to find at all, and before the surgeon was able to remove it, he drained more than four litres of fluid from it. Four litres! That's two huge milk cartons I was carrying around! Is it any wonder I lost eight kilos in one day! And I woke to discover I lost my ovary and my gall bladder too. I don't want to sound ungrateful. I'm truly grateful for what I believe was life-saving surgery, but I do remember thinking, 'You took my ovary? I don't remember saying you could have that.'

But a missing ovary was the least of my worries. The doctor came to visit me that afternoon on the ward when I was recovering from surgery. My colleague's wife, the neonatal nurse, had been looking after Sienna while I was operated on. She had brought Sienna to the hospital to see me; Sienna just six weeks old. And the doctor explained that the cyst had ruptured, had been oozing through my system for a while and that I would have to wait for the pathology results before discussing the next move. And I asked him, 'So what are you saying? Worst-case scenario…chemotherapy?' The doctor looked at me, he looked down at Sienna and then back at me. He put a kind hand on my shoulder and said, 'Let's just wait for the results.' I realise now that he couldn't say what he was truly thinking. He couldn't look at this woman with her new baby in her arms and tell her that the cyst had leaked throughout her system and that if indeed it was malignant, she was fucked. She was going to die.

But I didn't die. Those test results came back and the cyst had been benign and I didn't die. I got to live and Sienna got to keep her mum. And there has to be a reason for that.

There's something else I remember about that afternoon, after the operation, after the doctor came around to discuss the surgery with me. Aunty Vera rang, and while I was talking to her with the hospital phone wedged between my shoulder and my ear, Sienna, propped up on my outstretched legs, gave me her very first smile.

15

I could write a chapter (a whole 'nother book no doubt) about Fuckhead. I could tell you about the incessant phone calls, the threatening text messages, the times he entered my house uninvited in a drunken rage, the rants about taking me to court so that he could have half my house. I could describe for you, in minute detail, the afternoon I found myself at the police station with a baby in my arms, too afraid to go home because he was going to climb through my window in the middle of the night and slice my throat and take my baby and put her on a plane back to Africa so that I'd never see her again. I could tell you about the most terrifying day of my life when I had to face him in court and beg the judge to issue a restraining order against the man who had reduced me to a shivering shadow of my former self. But I don't want to waste another word on Fuckhead. Suffice to say he took my money and ran, and I was left holding the baby.

But you saw that coming, didn't you?

Instead, let me try and walk you through the nightmarish years that followed Sienna's arrival. I promise to be as accurate as I can, but in the scrapbooks of my mind, these are the dark ages, and memories are sketchy.

So Sienna must have been three, four months old. We were staying at Catherine's place, a friend I had made since starting work at Bathurst High School. My insomnia was still raging and my GP had increased the dose of Zyprexa, but I was afraid to take it while I was alone in the house with Sienna, so I asked Catherine if I could stay with her. She'd gone to bed. Sienna was asleep in the bed next to me, both of us in the spare room next to Catherine's. But I was broken, too far gone, and the drugs wouldn't work. I couldn't get to sleep.

I called out, 'Catherine?'

'Yeah, mate?'

'I need to go to the hospital.'

'OK.'

It was late. We must have put Sienna in the car and Catherine drove me. She must have spent the night with my baby. I don't remember. My mum drove down from Queensland the next day and I suppose my baby must have changed hands, but I don't remember.

I do remember hearing the triage nurse tell the doctor, 'She has a new baby at home. She says she doesn't feel safe,' and detecting a knowing nod between them. They moved me to a ward and gave me more drugs, something that finally knocked me out for a couple of hours and I woke, my mum there.

And then they transferred me to Panorama, saying the name as though I knew what that meant. Panorama? That's a mountain where they race cars isn't it? It's a type of photograph. What the fuck was Panorama? I soon found out it was a holding yard for the mentally ill until they were properly assessed and relocated.

I remember a white room. I remember a stainless steel mirror. I remember a nurse in a blue uniform with 'New South Wales Health' embroidered on the pocket. I remember my pants hanging loosely around my hips as I undid my belt and handed it over to her. And I remember her saying, 'I'll need your shoelaces too.'

I remember every minute seemed like an hour. I remember walking in circles around the common room, watching the clock and marvelling at the excruciating slowness of time. It was like being in labour all over again. I remember thinking that. And I remember the nurses pottering around on the other side of a thick glass pane, watching me, I imagine, like some strange experiment, like some rabid animal.

And I've tried describing the terror. In between admissions and since then, I've tried to find the words to describe it but I just can't. My mind cracked. All I knew was round-the-clock terror. Like gunpoint terror. Like waking up to find yourself buried alive in a coffin terror. I was off balance, seeing things and hearing things, strange voices whispering and whipping in my ears.

Sleep became a mystery, a magic trick. I chased it and chased it but could never catch it. I'd lie down and close my eyes but all I could hear was my blood pulsing in my ears. My guts were swimming, my frame was shrinking, my whole body seemed to levitate with terror, the skin on my arms lifting off the bone.

And then the dark thought, on a film before my eyes, on a loop. Me, arms swept out wide, legs poised, like a dancer, launching into the empty air socket before an oncoming train. Inhaling the smell and the taste of the metal tracks, feeling the blissful slam.

Just to get to sleep.

Some of the nurses were so vile, but I remember a kind one, Tracey. I can remember asking her, 'What's happening to me?'

And there were tears in her eyes. 'You've had a massive depressive episode, Jude.' They don't call it a nervous breakdown any more.

I saw a psychiatrist. He prescribed Effexor, Seroquel, Lord knows what else they were feeding me. But I wasn't getting better. I lived within walking distance of the hospital and I would go home in the day to find my poor mother floundering, an elderly woman with a baby to look after. I'd return to the hospital distraught, missing my baby, feeling guilty about Mum, wanting to die. Eventually, they suggested I stop going home.

They sent me to a hospital in Sydney, a post-natal ward at St John of God. It was a place for mothers and their babies, so Sienna came with me and my mum went back home to Queensland. I took their drugs and attended their cognitive behaviour therapy workshops and I even sat in the chapel some days and prayed. But I didn't sleep. And I didn't get better. And Sienna got reflux, screaming and screaming for two days until we figured out what it was. And I got mastitis, my breasts beetroot purple, too sore to even touch, but the nurses made me express and my body ached with fever. And the nurses wouldn't let me out of their sight. I was such a suicide risk, I wasn't even allowed to take my daughter for a walk around the block in her stroller and they asked me again and again, 'Do you have thoughts of hurting your baby?' And I told them truthfully, horrified, 'No! Never!' She was a gift, a delicate, sacred creature, no way in the world would I ever hurt her. But I wanted to give her away. I wanted to give her to someone who could take better care of her than I could.

And it's all such a blur. I wasn't right, I wasn't well, but I'd been there a month and they sent me home. And I wasn't sleeping but I tried to get back to life, I tried going back to work, taking Sienna to daycare and taking my medication and drowning myself with alcohol nightly. And still not sleeping.

And I remember I went to Orange to meet with Dr Phillip Boyce. I don't know when it was, or how old Sienna was and I can't even remember who organised the appointment for me. But that man spent three hours with me. There were other medical practitioners in the room as well, other women I think, but I can barely remember what we talked about. I think he made me walk through the story of the birth and I know I didn't sit down, for three hours, I paced and trembled and rocked my baby. And then he spoke those words that nobody else had said to me: post-traumatic-stress-disorder. PTSD.

And I still had miles to travel, but I turned a tiny corner that day. I knew that whatever was wrong with me, it was more than just depression. I knew depression. When I'd been depressed in the past, I could barely get out of bed. This was different. The terror and the insomnia. At least now I had a reason for it. And it felt like a relief.

He also told me that in some cases, Effexor could make patients worse. The psychiatrists at Panorama just kept upping the dose until I was on the maximum. Now Dr Boyce told me that I should stop taking it. I had to wean off it gradually, but even so, it was like withdrawing from heroin, my body sick and a sensation like electric shocks going off in my head. When I moved, it seemed my brain was bobbing up and down in a bowl of water.

Months passed. I tried to go back to work, just working part-time, but I wasn't coping. I wasn't sleeping. I was a trembling bag of bones. I took more time off, packing up the car and heading north to stay with Mum, there only a couple of days before she checked me in to a postnatal ward in Brisbane, the Belmont Hospital.

At Belmont Hospital, I met Dr Lyndal White. Finally, a woman who could see I was walking dead anyway and wasn't afraid to bring out the big guns. She completely bombed me with Seroquel and Zyprexa and Dothep and Escitalopram, maximum doses of everything. I rattled when I walked but she finally got me sleeping. It was protocol for patients to sleep with their babies in the room with them, but Dr White instructed the nurses to give me my medication at night, take Sienna to the other end of the ward and let me sleep. And I still had miles to walk, but at least if I was sleeping, I thought, perhaps there was a chance that I might actually start to heal.

Dr White also administered ECT, electroconvulsive-therapy. Every other day, they would take me around to the theatre, make me bite down on a rubber rod and put me under anaesthetic. I'd wake up with the most distressing amnesia that could last for hours, and for years after this treatment, my memory was rooted. In fact, it's never fully recovered. Neural pathways that are damaged by ECT can't be repaired, but the brain can create new pathways. I absolutely hated ECT, and to promote a better seizure, the anaesthetist would put ketamine in the anaesthetic. I would spend the day after treatment crawling the halls of the psych ward, tripping off my tree. I begged Dr White to stop the treatments and after about a dozen rounds, she finally agreed.

Dr White's conversations with me also took a different approach to the other doctors who had tried to treat me. Instead of making me talk about Fuckhead and the pregnancy and the birth and the pain, she asked me to talk about Ashlie. She took me back to the paddock on that cool autumn afternoon. She walked me to the highway. She made me hear the noise of the traffic, smell the scent of the car exhausts, watch my baby sister step out in front of that vehicle and meet her tragic end. And she made me turn to myself, the little girl in jeans and grubby shirt and dusty sneakers who shouldn't have been there. And she made me say to her, 'Jude, I forgive you.'

I was at Belmont for a long time, maybe two months. I know Sienna turned one while we were there. And that was scary, because I knew the post-natal ward didn't take women with babies older than one. After Sienna turned one, if I still wasn't well, I'd be treated by the system as just run-of-the-mill mental rather than specifically post-natal nuts. When I checked out, I told the nurses I wasn't sure I'd made any improvement. They actually laughed. 'Jude,' they said, 'are you serious? When you arrived, you were virtually catatonic. You have definitely improved.'

But still I had a long way to go. Some days were slightly better than others, but most days were hell. I had gained a lot of weight being on the antipsychotics and antidepressants, which I found really distressing, so if I felt I was half coping for more than five minutes, I'd try going off them, but I always ended up falling apart, unable to sleep and back in front of my wonderful GP, needing to up the doses again. Even now, almost nine years after Sienna was born, I take substantial amounts of psychiatric medication. I've come to accept that I'll never be off them, and I've stopped trying. The nightmare of psychosis just isn't worth it.

Sadly, Sienna's first six years mark the darkest days of my life and my most difficult battle with alcohol yet. I know how incredibly selfish and how insanely obvious this must sound, but I can remember one day, sitting on the couch watching Sienna playing with some toys, babbling in her baby talk on a mat on the floor. And I remember a thought struck me like a bolt out of the blue, so sudden and profound I could actually hear the words being spoken in my head. 'Jude,' the voice said, 'you realise, no one is coming to pick her up.' And that sounds ridiculous, but it took me so long to come to that understanding, that becoming a mother wasn't just a game, nor was it something that might come to an end when my daughter reached a certain age. This was it, this decision was irreversible, and unlike all the other decisions I'd made in my life that I didn't want to deal with, there'd be no running away from it this time. My selfish desires, my need for space, my craving for control over every aspect of my life no longer mattered. It was all about Sienna now. And for at least the first six years of Sienna's life, it felt like a prison sentence.

My life had turned into groundhog day. I'd get up, get Sienna ready for daycare, go to work, pick Sienna up from daycare, put her to bed and then sit in front of the television, sinking glass after glass of wine, until I'd either run out of wine or pass out. I could drink two, three bottles of wine every night of the week. I'd wake up in hell, depression so heavy it felt like the paws of a tiger on my chest. I'd get up, sink a few coffees and promise myself that day I wouldn't drink. But before the sun had set I was back at it again. I was on autopilot. My car didn't seem to be able to drive past the liquor store without turning in.

I can remember another epiphany from those early days that probably sounds completely stupid and obvious. Sienna was still in nappies. She'd been really unsettled, crying all day and I was changing her nappy for what felt like the millionth time. I looked down at her, wriggling and mewling on the baby change table, and I thought about myself as a baby, so innocent and helpless, entirely dependent on the sacrifices of another for my survival. And I realised that that person had been my mother.

Having Sienna forced me to see how selfish I was. She taught me to look at my own mother in a completely different light. Until then, I'd expected my mother to be there for me, to always place my needs before her own, even as an adult. And sure, she's made some mistakes, she hasn't always stepped up, but I realised then how she was more than just a mother. She was a human, with a life of her own, with her own history, her own needs and wants and her own faults and vulnerabilities. With her own story. And I realise now that even the most squirrel-shit-nutty-anything-but-perfect mother has made enormous sacrifices for her children. Sienna taught me, finally, to be truly grateful for this woman, this teacher, this carer, this counsellor, this giver of life and unconditional love.

My mother.

16

On Sienna's fourth birthday, I woke with yet another hangover. Sienna woke, ridiculously excited to open her presents; a dress-up outfit and some costume jewellery, and a waterproof Dora doll that did backstroke in the bathtub. There was also a package at the front door from her cousin: an Elsa doll that sang 'Let it Go' when you pressed on her heart.

It was a Friday, and I had to go to work and Sienna would spend the day at daycare. I sent her off with birthday cupcakes, topped with pink icing and sprinkles. And I went to work and sobbed, inconsolably, the entire day. My colleagues even had to cover some of my classes, I was such a mess.

My head teacher and good friend, Leeanne, held my hand and asked me, 'What is it?'

I looked at her through bloodshot eyes in a crumpled face. 'She's only four,' I cried.

I'd organised a party for her that afternoon in the beer garden of a family friendly hotel. All my workmates came, many of them bringing their own children. I'd organised a cake, a Minion princess cake, with chocolate icing and a decorative tiara. The guests sang 'Happy Birthday', Sienna blew out her candles and everybody ate a slice of cake. Then the kids went out to the playground, slipping down the slides and swinging on the swings, the dusty bark beneath the playground equipment turning their white school socks red. And the adults sat around, enjoying a few Friday afternoon drinks.

I had glass of wine after glass of wine, throwing them back so fast the shiraz barely touched the sides. I was completely plastered, barely able to walk myself to the bathroom. As the afternoon progressed and all the guests had left, I had to leave my car in the car park and Sienna and I climbed in to a cab to make our way home, where I put Sienna in a bath and got her in bed, then continued to drink until I passed out. I woke, a couple of hours later, in the middle of the lounge room floor. As I lifted my throbbing head, I felt something wet and sticky on the side of my face. Propping myself up on my hands, I could see whatever it was had soaked my shirt. It was vomit. I'd passed out and vomited all over myself, there on the lounge room floor.

There was no more denying it. My alcoholism was out of control and my life had become completely unmanageable. I was working with a daily hangover, so self-conscious about reeking of stale alcohol that I would stand back when my colleagues spoke to me. I looked a wreck, my skin blotchy, my face bloated, the whites of my eyes threaded with red veins. I was running like a rat on a wheel, so trapped in my addiction I wanted to die.

There was absolutely no joy in my life. I'd completely lost interest in all the things I liked to do. Some of my frustrated friends even became angry with me, lecturing me on my pathetic self-pity and inability to enjoy the role of motherhood. 'Look at her, Jude,' they'd tell me, unable to comprehend my misery. 'She's absolutely gorgeous. She's healthy and happy and she adores you. You're so lucky!' But I couldn't see it.

I knew the drinking had to stop. I seemed to be able to avoid alcohol, or at least, rein it in a little, when I wasn't working, but the stress of teaching full-time on top of single motherhood was unbearable. I knew that drastic measures needed to be taken. In a move that shocked and appalled my colleagues, I resigned from my permanent teaching position.

I taught up until the end of the term and then it was Easter break. I put Sienna and our new German shepherd, Stella, in the car, and we headed north, to Mum's, indefinitely. We split the drive in two, stopping at a hotel on the way, Sienna swimming in the hotel pool, me, sitting poolside watching her, sinking a six-pack of beer.

When I arrived at Mum's, I cried and cried. Mum made me a tea and we sat on her back porch, me so distraught Mum actually gave me a valium. And I got on the internet and punched into Google, 'AA meeting – Bribie Island'. And it just so happened there was an AA meeting that very night.

I cried and cried my way through my first AA meeting; huge, embarrassing sobs that seemed to explode from the core of my soul. And I sat and listened to a room full of complete strangers telling their stories, horrific stories of men losing their wives and mothers losing their children and people being disowned by their families and losing their jobs and going to prison. And all of them spoke about their ongoing journey with recovery. And all of them sounded so wise and so humble. And none of them even batted an eyelid at the woman sobbing hysterically at the end of the table, other than the odd person who squeezed my shoulder kindly when they walked past. The energy, the presence of collective kindness and compassion was truly palpable.

At the end of the meeting, a couple of women came up to me and introduced themselves, giving me their number. I went home, still desperate with guilt and remorse and self-loathing, but that night, for the first time since I could remember, there was the tiniest flicker of hope. If the people I had just met in that room tonight had hit rock bottom and returned, maybe so too could I. I'd seen and felt something like redemption in that room. And I wanted it.

I stayed at Mum's for quite a few weeks. I took Sienna to the beach, and pushed her on the swings in the park, and I went shopping with my mum and helped her cook chicken curry and spaghetti bolognese, and I went to every AA meeting for the remaining weeks I stayed at Mum's. And I still cried. And I still felt guilty, and I still hated myself and I still felt like I was absolutely insane. But I didn't drink.

When I went home, I started going to meetings in Bathurst. For the next twelve months, Sienna would bring her headphones and sit in the corner playing games on my phone while I sat for hours, listening to a room full of recovering alcoholics telling their story, and telling them mine. And I learnt that sucking on a bottle every time I was unable to 'do life on life's terms' was no different to a toddler spitting the dummy and screaming on the floor of a supermarket aisle. And I learnt that I was lying when I told myself that the only one I hurt through my drinking was me. And I met some beautiful people and I made some beautiful friends. And I was blessed with the gift of recovery.

One day at a time.

17

When I think about the way any of us look back on our lives, I imagine standing on the top of a high mountain. There's a bag at our feet, and the view from the top of the mountain depends on which pair of glasses we pull out of the bag and put over our eyes.

When I stand on the mountain with dark coloured glasses on and look back over my life, the path I've trodden is riddled with potholes and sharp dunes, stretching out into the distance where the horizon meets storm-clouded skies. I see the trauma of watching my sister die, I see the violence of my family's destruction, I see the disappointment of lost love, I see the pain and despair of my battle with poor health, I see the madness of my illness, I see the loneliness of my addiction. I see a world of intolerance and poverty and injustice. I see war and disease and senseless death. I hear the cries of neglected children, the despondency of the displaced, the brutality of the forces of nature. I can turn my head and look the other way, towards the path stretched out before me. It's shrouded in thick fog that looks, from my position here on the top of the mountain, completely impenetrable. I see the misery of old age and sickness, I see the fear of loss of independence, I see the inevitability of bereavement, I see the cycle of self-loathing, I see the pointlessness of regret, I feel the weight of my responsibilities and I see, most terrifying of all, the uncertainty of my daughter's future.

But I can take those dark coloured glasses off. I can reach into the bag and pick out another pair of glasses, and I can stand on this same mountain and see the view through a totally different lens. I can look back over my life and see the path I've trodden is a road paved with gold, stretching back to where the horizon meets cloudless blue skies. I see the joy of my childhood. I see my mother and Ashlie and I holding hands and dancing in a circle to Kamahl's 'It's a Small World After All' in the lounge room of our family home. I see the blue twinkle of my father's eyes reflecting the dancing flames of the campfire as he holds his beer and sings me a sad ballad, his voice clear and sweet, 'The war ship had landed, and I came ashore'. I see the beauty in the simplicity of walking around Aunty Vera's garden as she shows me her carefully attended flower beds splashing colour around the yard. I feel the exhilaration of the wind in my hair as I gallop through the bush on one of my beautiful horses. I feel the unconditional love and loyalty of my dogs. I feel the joy of escape, in books, in films, in music, in nature. I feel the accomplishment of singing one of my original songs. I feel the care and protection and respect and laughter of my world full of beautiful friends. I feel the thrill of love. And lust. I feel the humility of the knowledge that my time here is fleeting. I feel the power in choosing to live. I feel the gratitude I have for the exquisite gift that is my daughter, the softness of her skin, the intelligence behind her eyes, the kindness of her heart and the indomitableness of her soul.

Sienna turns nine in a couple of weeks. She's having a slumber party, a group of her school friends are coming to camp in a tent in our backyard. She's made the party invitations all by herself, her abundance of creative energy already shining through in the language she uses and the images she's arranged all over the page.

Wayne will come to Bathurst. He will bring his daughter, who is almost Sienna's age, and he'll help me pitch the tent and light a fire in a bucket and we'll roast marshmallows and Wayne will have a beer and I will make a pot of tea because I don't drink any more and I'll bring out my guitar and Sienna will sing along to all the songs we sing together. And then she'll ask me, like she always does, to play the song I wrote for her, her gorgeous face looking up at me with love, and pride and expectation: her teacher, her protector, her role model.

Her mother.

And of course, I'll sing it for her, like I always do…

Come into my arms, 'cause baby you show me the world
Trace the lines on my palms that will tell you the story of a girl
Lay your head on my chest and remember the way you came to be
You're gonna need some rest love, if you're here to rescue me.

www.ingramcontent.com/pod-product-compliance
Lightning Source LLC
Chambersburg PA
CBHW030911080526
44589CB00010B/254